The Secret of *half-arsed* Parenting

This book is for my kids, who are proud of it,
even though there are lots of stories about them in it.
For Paddy, for his love and support.
And for my mum Jen and dad Mick, who are the original –
and best – half-arsed parents.

Published in 2021 by Murdoch Books, an imprint of Allen & Unwin

Murdoch Books Australia
83 Alexander Street, Crows Nest NSW 2065
Phone: +61 (0)2 8425 0100
murdochbooks.com.au
info@murdochbooks.com.au

Murdoch Books UK
Ormond House, 26–27 Boswell Street, London WC1N 3JZ
Phone: +44 (0) 20 8785 5995
murdochbooks.co.uk
info@murdochbooks.co.uk

 A catalogue record for this book is available from the National Library of Australia

A catalogue record for this book is available from the British Library

ISBN 978 1 76052 573 6 Australia
ISBN 978 1 91163 274 0 UK

Cover design by Alissa Dinallo
Text design by Susanne Geppert
Cover photography by Getty Images, Foodcollection

Typeset by Midland Typesetters, Australia
Printed and bound in Australia by Griffin Press

10 9 8 7 6 5 4 3 2 1

The Secret of *half-arsed* Parenting

DR SUSIE O'BRIEN

murdoch books
Sydney | London

CONTENTS

INTRODUCTION
THE HALF-ARSED WAY

Parenting sure isn't what it used to be.

When I was growing up in the 70s, kids were free-range, like the underarm hair. Babies spent hours in the backyard, gazing at the clouds from their wooden gaols. Toddlers tottered around shopping centres on leashes like dogs. Mums switched to menthol cigarettes when they were pregnant, and dads dipped their baby's dummies in whiskey to help them sleep through the night.

By the 80s, parents continued to walk the fine line between neglect and indifference. Kids had latchkeys and let themselves in after school, rolled around unsecured in the back seats of cars and sat in the car park of the local pub. Their parents, who were inside drinking, occasionally brought them out packets of chips and lemonade. (Okay, that might have just been my sister and me.)

In the 90s, mobile phones made their debut. But they weren't smart, nor were most parents, who didn't yet have Google to help them with their kids' homework. Back then, peanut-butter sandwiches were still sold in tuckshops, kids had lemonade stands without needing council permits, and internet connections dropped out when you picked up the landline.

Things have improved. These days kids wear seatbelts, nuts are banned in schools and babies don't wake up with hangovers, but it's harder than ever to be a parent. Now lunchbox food has to be nude, Baa Baa is a rainbow sheep and we're meant to ask permission from a baby before changing its nappy. Children used to be seen and not heard, now they're noisy and everywhere. Kids today – even the bratty ones – are indulged and adored. 'Look, he spoke a word. Whip out your iPhone and record it for posterity.' 'Look, he's preciously pooing. Film it for his 21st.' 'Look, she finished last in a 50 metre walking race. Better give her a medal.'

I've been a parent for 17 years now, but I've got more questions than ever. How can my elder son get an A in trigonometry but still think 'verse' is a verb? (As in, 'Will the Sydney Swans *verse* Geelong today?') And how does my 14-year-old know the difference between an infusion and a reduction, thanks to TV cooking shows, but not know how to grill us sausages for dinner? And why did they spend their time in Covid lockdown killing each other on video games instead of nurturing a sourdough starter like the kids of my Instagram friends?

It's time to do things differently and embrace the half-arsed approach to raising kids that served our parents so well. We need to stop being hyper-parents, helicopter parents or hands-on parents and instead become half-arsed parents.

Half-arsed parenting is about doing half as much and knowing it is still more than enough. It's not an invitation to give up and do a bad job across the board. It doesn't mean giving kids less love, empathy or protection. It means releasing yourself from other people's standards, expectations and rules.

Half-arsed parents know that when it comes to raising kids, you don't have to be perfect. Know your limits and set the bar low enough so you succeed. Near-enough is usually good enough. It's okay that your child's first word was 'Bluey' or 'Elsa' rather than 'Mama' or 'Dadda'. Because here's the truth:

No one cares as much as you about the way
you're bringing up your kids.
They may act as if they do, but they don't. Trust me.

This means it's okay to fake it until you make it. And if you don't make it, no one will notice. The celebrities pretending to be perfect are faking it too. They spend their days posting inspirational phrases like 'Be the best you #glow, #bless' but only get out of bed thanks to a generous slug of vodka in their green goddess breakfast smoothie. I am not green or a goddess. I once tried to drink hot water with lemon and it looked like a giant cup of wee. I also made a kale smoothie and it tasted like grass clippings. Half-arsed parents know the kids will be alright, like they always are. What's important is that mums and dads are alright too.

Half-arsed parenting is also about getting back to basics. Whatever happened to toasted sandwiches for dinner? Kids sharing bedrooms and bathrooms? Making meals with what you've got, not what you buy from the organic market or get delivered via an app? That's how it was when we were young and we turned out okay, didn't we? (Yes, except for our record-high anxiety rates and inexplicable love of TV reality dating shows.)

This book will help you uncover the absurdities and hypocrisies of modern parenting and show how they make mums and dads feel guilty for doing normal things. It pokes fun at all the unrealistic goals and expectations thrust on parents today. Parents don't need more thrusting: it's how we got into this mess in the first place. Half-arsed parents love their kids, but find raising them harder than it should be, mainly due to the interference of others. Mums and dads already know the answers and should trust their instincts to get it right. We should not be shamed for using cling wrap on school sandwiches, letting our kids read *Thomas the Tank Engine* even though there are no female lead characters, or neglecting them during home schooling so we could get some work done.

As a result of all this pressure and guilt, parents feel compelled to be more invested in their kids' lives than ever before. It's not just about protecting kids from unseen and often non-existent dangers, but caring about every grade, interaction and conversation. This means attending every sporting match, manipulating every friendship and orchestrating all aspects of school life.

It wasn't like that when I was young. Spending weekends watching me exhibit my dire lack of athletic skills wasn't high on Mick O'Brien's agenda. He had better things to do, like wearing budgie smugglers as daywear and cementing things into the ground. I can't imagine Dad – or even Mum – putting love notes in my lunchbox, capturing every sporting move on camera or giving me veggies fanned out like a rainbow for dinner like parents are expected to do today.

This book will let you feel good about dropping your standards. It is needed because these days, parenthood is not just another job. It's become a quasi-religious calling, requiring nothing less than 100 per cent devotion, 100 per cent of the time.

This book is for parents and the grandparents, friends and family members trying to keep them sane. It's for the stay-at-home mums who consider a trip to the doctor special 'me time', and think wandering through a supermarket without kids is better than therapy. It's for the working mums hoping the black rings under their eyes are last night's make-up rather than their middle-aged mummy face. It's for the dads who work their arses off all day and then get frowned at by their bosses because they leave on time to get their kids from childcare. It's also for the nannas and pops wondering where everyone's manners have gone.

Signs of hyper-parenting are all around us, particularly in the middle classes where people have the time and resources to obsess about how their kids' lives are measuring up. Psychologist and author Michael Carr-Gregg told me recently about some 'quite anxious' parents he met at a kindergarten in a well-off suburb. 'The main things they wanted to know were about what sort of toys their boys and girls should be playing with – should they go with Mother Nature or should they decide for them?' he said. 'And they wanted to know if their child was going to be good enough at maths and English.' Welcome to modern parenting, where parents are sweating the small stuff.

Kids are so used to their parents doing everything for them that they've lost confidence in their own abilities. Carr-Gregg says it's a case of parents trying to make their kids' lives easier by fixing problems, handing them opportunities and being their full-time cheerleader. 'It's driven by guilt. Parents are so busy running their lives and paying off the mortgage that they give their children money rather than time,' he says. It's no wonder kids are fatter than ever. We're doing all the running around, not them. One in four children is overweight or obese, according to the latest Australian Government health data – this is three times more than 30 years ago. The kids of today don't get outside enough, spend too much time in front of screens, eat too much crap and spend their childhoods strapped into the back seat of a car.

Despite all this, and even during a global pandemic, there are lots of good things going on. Australians have never lived as long, been as healthy overall or led such prosperous lives. In general, our houses are bigger, our jobs better paid and our lives more comfortable compared to past generations. Things many of us take for granted, like overseas travel, high levels of credit and huge houses, were unthinkable even 30 years ago. There are some key exceptions – such as those from Indigenous backgrounds and those with disabilities – but most Australians are better off than ever before.

There's also more acceptance of different types of families, which is another good thing. Australian Institute of Family Studies (AIFS) data shows that by the age of 17, only 53 per cent of kids live with both biological parents. This includes one in five children with step-families who 'experience complex living arrangements'. You know, families where Christmas lunch involves dad and his new wife, their two kids, her kids from a former relationship, as well as their mum, her new partner, his kids and their kids. Throw in in-laws, out-laws and drunk old Uncle Harold, and you've got a very complicated scenario. The Real Insurance Family Values report shows many people are happy to see parents no longer staying together for the sake of the kids and they don't feel outraged against past taboos such as interracial marriage and teen pregnancy.

Families are changing in other ways too. Same-sex marriage is now legal. Babies can be made using three parents via IVF. And there's greater acceptance of sexual diversity. I see the term 'parent' as covering all types of people: mums or dads who are married, de-facto, single or not sure. They might be heterosexual, pansexual or gay. They might be someone who writes their own gender descriptor on government forms, gender-fluid, intersex, non-binary. It doesn't matter. We're all in this together.

Yet increased health and wealth and greater social acceptance isn't making us content, with one in five parents saying they were happier before they had children. I find that extraordinary. Aren't kids meant to make us feel complete? Fulfilled? Ecstatic? That's the parenting dream we're sold. So why do half of all parents say they don't even know how they feel about having children and are neither more nor less happy than before? We love our kids; it's parenting we struggle with.

This book will help you explore why parenting today has become so toxic. Even better, it will help you work out what to do about it. For a long time, we've needed a new model of raising kids that takes the stress off kids and parents and lets us all enjoy life again. Here it is. Be ready to free yourself as a parent. Let go of hyper-parenting, helicopter parenting and hands-on parenting and embrace half-arsed parenting – it's cheeky, but it works. Read on, and be prepared to do things differently.

PART ONE

Becoming Half-Arsed

Chapter 1

HALF-ARSED PARENTING BASICS

Modern parents are chock-full of guilt. Right now, the dog's giving me daggers, I haven't been to the gym, the kids haven't done their homework and dinner is UberEats butter chicken with extra garlic naan. Again. Confession time: sometimes I drape washing on the line without using pegs, or put clothes in the dryer even though it's sunny outside. I've also been known to skip pages of my kids' school readers on purpose so I can get them to bed faster, and during home schooling I sacked myself as my son's teacher by 9.30 am on the first day. A study by social researchers The Korn Group found Aussie mums want to feel sexy, appreciated and happy. Instead, we often feel overwhelmed and guilty, craving 'mum breaks' that involve chocolate and/or wine. Right on. We find motherhood rewarding but also have a car that smells 'like a day-old lunchbox' and treats stashed away in our cupboards.

Dads face the same pressures. They want to be home with their kids more, but feel pressured to excel at work, which often involves long hours. They'd love to be home earlier, but don't want to be frowned upon for slacking off at work. Many dads don't feel appreciated either. Fathers want recognition that they're not idiots babysitting their kids, and confirmation that their 'signature dad spag bog' is actually the best in the world. (It often is.)

This book is here to help take the pressure down, let go of the guilt and give you permission to raise your kids the way you want to, not the way you think you have to.

Ditch the guilt

Letting go of guilt is bloody hard. As a full-time working mother, I've got gallons of the stuff, but I hang out with people who understand me rather than judge me. My pals and I are more likely to swap stories and laugh about our failings rather than pretend to be Prozac-perfect. We smuggle a bottle of wine into the dry-zone local park for mothers' group, let the kids push themselves on swings, count French fries as a vegetable and ignore screaming children unless there's blood. If they're screaming, they're breathing; remember that. I understand the guilt that propels many parents, but I don't let it keep me awake at night. (In fact, nothing keeps me awake since I bought those noise-cancelling headphones.)

Most hands-on parents will tell you they've got a running sheet looping through their head at all times: *look up date of swimming carnival, buy new bathers, check for nits, find nits, buy nit cream, remember Nanna's birthday, buy present for Nanna, go around and see Nanna* . . . It's called the third shift: the emotional labour that has to be done in families. While some men do it, it's a thankless task that mostly falls to women.

An internal monologue is constantly running in my head. *Where are the kids? Should I be picking them up? What time does soccer start? When does ballet finish? What ballet is she doing this term? What kid? What term? AAAHHH!* The Korn Group found that while mothers clearly revel in motherhood, they also long for their 'freewheeling days' before kids. 'They recognise they can't do everything perfectly but still feel judged by others,' director Neer Korn says. I get it. Sixteen years on, my kids still judge me for not having a two-storey house and an in-ground swimming pool like some of the other kids in our mothers' group.

Guilty mums conclude they should spend more hands-on time with their children, not less. They sacrifice their own social lives to make more time for their kids, which often leads to resentment and more guilt. Many also end up doing less paid work. Doing less parenting doesn't seem to occur to anyone. Or if it does, they keep it to themselves, knowing they'd be seen as terrible mothers.

Guilt is such a worthless emotion. It leads people to make choices based on what they believe others think they should do rather than what they want to do. Guilt is caused by a mismatch between reality and desire. It's a common trap of modern parenthood that's created entirely by us. Sure, there are many brands, products and industries fuelling this guilt, but we're the ones who let them dictate how we feel. This means parents end up questioning what they do and how they do it, but they don't question the guilt that makes them feel like crap in the first place. And they don't see doing less parenting as an option. Why the hell not? Less is more, or it should be.

Half-arsed parents do less of the intense, overprotective parenting that takes up so much time and energy. They also give themselves a break rather than rely on others to give them permission to feel okay about themselves. It is about keeping it real and having a laugh rather than judging others and yourself. If you're the kind of parent (and I know a few) who ruffles up the edges of cupcakes so the school mummy mafia thinks they're home-baked, then you need a reality check. The problem is your choice of friends, not your baking skills. Find some friends who don't catalogue your failings but greet you at the door with a bottle of champers and a store-bought sponge. And make sure you apply the three-second rule to everything that gets dropped. This includes ice creams, dummies and Daddy's pants. (Now you're a parent, three seconds is all you'll get.)

You do have time

It would be easy to curl up in the foetal position on the couch for a few hours – or years. All this hyper-parenting has made parents so over-stretched, they don't have time to live their own lives. One study from the Parenting Research Centre found between a third and a half of all mums and dads struggle to find the time to regularly play with their kids inside or outside. Parents also say they are too busy to catch up with friends, spend one-on-one time with children or sit around the dinner table for a home-cooked meal. I often feel the same way.

However, other studies show parents do have time: it's a question of how they spend it. The latest time-use data from the National Centre for Social and Economic Modelling (NATSEM) shows Australians have 20 per cent of their day to spend on leisure and recreational pursuits. The report even calls our spare time 'generous'. Netflix is going gangbusters in this country, we're on our phones for hours at a time, there are record attendances at sporting matches and online shopping is more popular than ever.

One conclusion is that parents are not as busy as they think they are. Parents are filling their days with things that take up their time and attention but don't make them happy or satisfied. Why is this? It's because they think that's what they have to do to be a good parent: enrol kids in endless activities, keep them inside where they are safe and praise them regardless of their achievements. Parents do have enough time to do the things they want; it's a question of how they use the hours they have and the choices they make.

The AMP NATSEM report on Australia's time use shows people have an average of five free hours on Sundays, four free hours on Saturdays and three and a half free hours each weekday. Despite this, 40 per cent of women and 30 per cent of men report being always rushed or pressed for time. This rises to eight out of ten women who work more than 40 hours a week. The main reason for this is family pressures, but also the 'inability to say no' – a trait suffered in equal measure by men and women, the AMP NATSEM report says. Hmmm, sounds familiar . . .

Downtime is important. I love a bit of Netflix, enjoy having a wine with friends and adore flicking through a mag on the couch. The latter usually lasts for 15 seconds before one of the kids yells out that they've run out of toilet paper and could I bring them some. We all need time off for ourselves. It's not desirable; it's essential. Half-arsed parents prioritise the things that matter to them as well, so everyone is happy, not only the kids. It's about saying no to another netball team or dance class that requires two sessions a week across town in an already packed family schedule. Making the kids do more around the house. Leaving work on time. Letting the dishes sit in the sink and going for a walk with a friend after dinner instead. Helping the kids become more independent and resilient. And buying toilet paper so you get more couch time.

Drop your standards

The idea that I would be a perfect parent was a euphoric fantasy that lasted about three days after my first son was born, thanks mainly to some very fine hospital drugs. This was replaced with a much more pragmatic 'she'll be right' attitude for child two, and 'lucky no one saw me do that' with child three. That's the half-arsed way. And you know what? No one's died. No one's psycho (except for me when my kids take my phone charger and don't return it). And the authorities haven't visited once.

I am a good enough parent. The phrase 'good enough mother' was first coined in 1971 by Donald Winnicott, a British paediatrician. He concluded that babies benefited when their mothers failed them in minor ways, such as not immediately grabbing them the minute they cried. He argued this made babies and kids able to survive and thrive in a world that doesn't always meet their needs. His approach has been deeply unpopular in recent years, but I'm on Team Winnicott. I am proud to be a good enough parent, not a perfect one. My kids are happier because I am happier. The more children I have, the more relaxed I get, because with each one my standards drop lower and lower.

With the first child, if you drop the dummy, you sterilise it on the stove. With the second, you run the dummy under the hot water tap. With the third, you lick it and put it back in their mouth. (That's if you notice at all.) The first-born gets an amazing birthday party with no expense spared and lavish gifts, the second gets a few friends over in the backyard, and the third gets Maccas and a supermarket sponge.

When the first child has activities, you stand breathless on the sidelines. For the second, you go if you can and for the third, you're lucky to remember when things are on, given that every weekend involves no fewer than 13 sporting matches, four birthday parties and two school events. Try getting through that lot with a hangover, and you quickly find the wheels falling off the parenting wagon. Anyone these days who has more than two kids is told, 'I don't know how you do it'. That usually means, 'I am sooo glad

I'm not you.' And, 'I'm not going to be the one to tell you you've got vomit in your hair, food on your top and a panty liner stuck to the back of your skirt.'

Half-arsed parenting is about doing what you can, not doing as much as you can to impress others who don't care and won't notice. There's a reason why third and fourth children are often more resilient – they have to be. When my third child was young, I only paid full attention to him when he was screaming or bleeding.

Half-arsed parents also don't assess their own success through their children's attainments. All of this time spent driving kids around, paying for activities and pumping up their egos means many parents are overly invested in their children's achievements. I'll bet you've all seen those ugly sporting parents on the sidelines, screaming because their daughter missed another goal or shouting at a footy umpire because of a call they didn't like.

My children's sports complex has issued new rules in a bid to curb the 'physical aggression' in non-contact indoor soccer matches played by kids as young as five. Parents and coaches are now formally told they must not 'raise issues of disagreement publicly', 'criticise opposing team members or supporters by word or gesture' or 'ridicule or yell at a child for making a mistake or losing a competition'.

Things are so bad that many sporting venues put up signs that say:

```
┌─────────────────────────────────────┐
│                                     │
│          PLEASE REMEMBER            │
│                                     │
│          These are kids             │
│        This is just a game          │
│       Coaches are volunteers        │
│        Umpires are human            │
│      It's not the World Cup         │
│                                     │
└─────────────────────────────────────┘
```

Following a nasty physical altercation between a parent and a umpire some years ago, umpires for my son's junior footy matches are now escorted on and off the grounds by parent volunteers. How's that for a sign of the times?

It's time to let it all go. Your son misses a goal. So what? He's probably not going to be the next Gary Ablett or Cristiano Ronaldo anyway. Can't make your daughter's concert rehearsal because you're having lunch with the girls? So what? School lunches are Vegemite sandwiches the kids make themselves and an apple that's not cut up? Who cares? Not them. And neither should you.

Greatest hits parenting

There are many good reasons why the 70s, 80s and even 90s are often seen as a high-water mark for childhood. We knew less, we cared less, we did less. These are the hallmarks of half-arsed parenting. When I was growing up in the 70s, we raised ourselves. We didn't have play dates; we played with all the kids in the neighbourhood and rode home when it got dark, not forgetting to grab some smokes for our parents from the shops on the way. We'd double-dink on our Malvern Star bikes (*Look Mum, no hands!*) and swing off the Hills Hoist to land on death-trap metal trampolines covered in dishwashing liquid. No helmets, no seatbelts and no gluten-free; it was life on the edge.

Back then, dads drove with one arm out the window and babies were strapped into bassinets that weren't strapped into cars. Mums would leave kids to forage in the fridge for dinner while they attended consciousness-raising groups and looked at their vaginas with mirrors. They stopped wearing make-up and started wearing T-shirts with slogans such as 'Every mother is a working woman' and 'Sisterhood is Powerful'. My sister and I didn't really mind about our mum Jen being a feminist, but we did think she should wear more lipstick.

Actor Rachel Griffiths has talked about raising her three kids, Banjo, Clementine and Adelaide, 70s style. 'Children are like dogs,' she told one interviewer. 'They really shouldn't be inside; they need to run and use their bodies.' She talked about her desire to recreate the era when 'your mother would yell, "Dinner!" and kids would come out of the creek or appear out of bushes'.

The 80s were similar. Acid-washed jeans replaced flares and poodle perms replaced Farrah Fawcett flicks, but life was still free and easy. Half-arsed parent, author and blogger Shannon Kelly White remembers this era fondly. She says she doesn't recall parents of the 80s being as uptight as many mums and dads today. 'They were too busy getting their hair permed and inflicting passive smoking on us to be bothered with trivial things like our safety and wellbeing,' White says in *Parenting for Legends*. Yeah, and serving their kids Spam and Tang for dinner without caring what anyone else thought.

Same for the 90s, when dial-up internet and a lack of social media kept a lid on kids' screen time and expectations. They watched TV rather than streaming shows on their phones, and pestered their parents about moving to *Beverly Hills 90210* like Brenda and Brandon. But most mums and dads didn't care what their kids thought. They were too busy worrying about the world ending thanks to the Y2K bug to give their kids medals for turning up to a sporting event, or put faces on their school lunches to seduce them into eating something healthy.

There are a few things around today that have improved our quality of life, like bike helmets, car seats, SPF30 sunscreen and laws that prohibit kids from stocking up on smokes at the corner store. Our lives were simpler back then, even though we didn't know it at the time. We didn't realise how lucky we were until we started raising our own kids in an era of wheat intolerances, indoor play centres and breakfast cereals with 25 ancient grains and more sugar than a can of Coke.

As parents, we aren't able to raise our kids the way we were brought up, even though we'd love to. The world has moved on, and many of the parenting practices of these past eras are now seen as lazy, crazy or neglectful. These days, more attention, love and praise are thought to be better, although there's much evidence to the contrary. We're also much more hands-on when we're at home with the kids to make up for the fact that we're now working more than our parents did.

This all means kids now are over-loved, over-protected and over-praised in ways we couldn't have imagined back then. The challenge for half-arsed parents is to do things differently. It's time for greatest hits parenting. Channel a bogan rock radio station and take the greatest hits of the 70s, 80s and 90s and combine them with the best of today.

For instance, many kids now have earbuds or headphones protecting them from outside noise or conversations about whose turn it is to unpack the dishwasher. Such impressive ways to avoid everyday family life didn't exist when I was growing up. Our children need to be taught to be more social, more communal and less individual, like kids had to be when there was just one screen in the house and no Bluetooth earbuds. It's not just a matter of different technology and different times, but a different way of doing things. Half-arsed parents will unplug kids from their screens and devices when *we* need it, not when *they* want it (which is never). We'll let them roam free and entertain themselves without monitoring them every second of the day. And we'll stop doing everything for them and praising their mediocrity.

I am not asking you to become an annoying hippie parent who brags about having a screen-free house, weekends full of meaningful nature-based activities and kids who can play for three hours with a pipe cleaner and a bit of earwax. These people are as bad as hyper-parents or helicopter parents – perhaps worse, because they think they're better than everyone else. They make other mums and dads feel like they're failing because their kids want perfectly normal things like the latest mobile phone models, Disney pyjamas and Maccas for dinner.

It's not like the 70s, 80s and 90s was all beer and skittles, or Moselle and Milo. One friend of mine says her mother sent her and her siblings out to play every Saturday and Sunday and then locked the doors to stop them from coming back in until it got dark. You don't hear hippie parents bragging about stuff like that.

Half-arsed parents are happy to take advantage of the tech advances of today's world – it might be letting the kids spend eight hours on their iPads to get through a long car trip or bribing them with wi-fi access to make them behave. There's nothing wrong with this. Greatest hits parenting does not require kids to look out the window at the scenery for hours or spend the weekend reading *Beano* annuals from the 40s before going to an art gallery. Half-arsed parents welcome the idea of doing a Cher and turning back time – but they know better than to foist their myopic misplaced nostalgia on their kids. Half-arsed parents don't have rose-coloured glasses. They watch *The Block* and know anything rose-coloured is *sooo* 2018.

Don't let the buggers smell your fear

Another piece in the half-arsed parenting puzzle is making sure the kids aren't in control. This can be the hardest thing to get right. I was reminded of this one Sunday afternoon when

I spent two hours at a freezing suburban footy ground acting as the volunteer water carrier for my kid's footy team. I stood there on the sidelines, running on to the field with the water bottles as soon as there was a break after a goal. Stay on too long and I could cost the team a point. Fail in my duties and someone might go thirsty. It was more pressure than it should have been. I stood there thinking, is this really what we've come to as parents? Lugging heavy bottles around a football field on the off-chance a 12-year-old needs a mouthful of water? 'I'm pretty sure no one was carrying water onto the field when I was a child,' my partner said. 'Make sure you don't muck it up, Mum,' my kid said.

It made me realise the inmates are running the asylum. In more than a decade of watching junior sports and activities, I've seen it all. Children targeting other kids on and off the field. Kids screaming at their parents because they're five minutes late or have the wrong shorts. Kids blatantly ignoring their coaches and other volunteer officials. Eight-year-olds sitting on a chair while their parents kneel in the mud to get their shoes on and off for them. At the end of it, the kids get a medal for participating, a hot dog and lolly snake from the canteen and a chauffeured drive home from mum or dad. What do the parents get? Dirty knees.

Not all kids are like this, but something is seriously out of whack. We are pushover parents raising a generation of pampered, privileged children. So much so that Aldi now sells screen-operated toddler exercise bikes in their famous middle aisle. The bikes allow kids to play games on their tablets while they ride in the comfort of their living rooms. No more outdoor exercise! No more free play! No need to ever leave the house! The reward for exercise is more screen time, not the pleasure that comes from being active.

Other parents feel the same pressure to please their kids, and it comes from even the youngest kids. 'I can't get him off the iPad,' says one parent of a two-year-old. The kid made such a fuss that the parent stopped trying. 'I can't get her to eat healthy food. All she wants is white bread jam sandwiches with the crusts cut off,' laments another. What these children want, they get, because their parents are too scared to stand up to them. These days, if a kid is screaming, people judge the parents, not the child. This is a big change from past decades, when kids were more likely to be seen as naughty. Now parents are seen as neglectful or abusive.

Now there are many kids who think nothing of interrupting an adult conversation because they want to say something. They blame their parents if they forget anything and they expect to always have the latest gadgets and fashion items, regardless of the cost. Kids today think they have rights we would never have dreamed of when growing up in the 70s, 80s and 90s. We're not empowering them, we're doing what Carr-Gregg calls 'infantilising them into incompetence'. Perhaps we should start by saying no a little more often, and get them to carry their own water bottles for a change.

We fought the kids, and the kids won

I'm not saying I've got it right myself – as a working mum who's raising three kids solo more than half the time, I know the guilt that comes from having to work long hours or struggling to keep up with the Joneses. One Sunday, I was driving one son to the bookshop to get the latest book in his favourite series before delivering him to a play date. Then I had to ferry my older two to their sporting matches, in each case dropping them an hour early for warm-up then coming back to watch their games and fulfil my volunteer duties. It was crazy, but that's what's expected of parents now. Too many of us give up our own weekends for our kids' activities and drop everything to meet their needs. We'd never forget Saturday ballet practice or football training, but we've forgotten to have a life of our own.

It reminds me of a disastrous trip to the snow when my oldest kids were two and four. Well actually, it was a trip to the grass because there was no snow. My kids were expecting snow and when they didn't get it, they turned into menopausal midgets. At lunch, they stuffed their faces with hot chips and picked fights with each other. At dinner, they each had a massive tantrum over my insistence they *share* a bottle of juice, which ended in my four-year-old lying face-down on the carpet in the restaurant, screaming like I'd removed his organs with a dinner fork.

My kids had an outrageous sense of entitlement, which turned them into toddler-sized terrorists the minute they didn't get what they wanted or expected. Surely they knew how lucky they were to go to the snow (even though there wasn't any) or eat in a restaurant?

I didn't ever do these things when I was growing up in the Western Australian bush. But they are part of a generation of kids for whom treats and special occasions have become commonplace. Parents work hard so we can give them the best we can afford – but we don't always think about the effect it may be having on them.

Parents are encouraged to go to ridiculous lengths to accommodate their bratty and pampered offspring. I remember hearing a few years ago about a two-year-old who ate nothing but yoghurt. He ate 14 tubs of the stuff a day. No fruit and veg, no meat – not even McDonald's chippies. Although it drove his parents crazy with worry, they were told to let him eat what he wanted because forcing the issue would stress *him* out. Another mother was so desperate to get her son to eat veggies that she concocted an elaborate game which required her to cook vegetables from the alphabet two different ways. She posted the results on a blog and it spawned a national craze in the UK. It appears that kids don't get told to eat what they're given or go hungry anymore.

Clearly, these kids – like mine on occasion – have got the upper hand. It's time for parents to back off, set some boundaries and book as many ski trips as they like for mid-summer without fearing the consequences.

Where's *my* participation medal?

A while ago, I was sitting at a suburban hall watching my daughter and her friends receive end-of-term certificates. A swarming paparazzi pack of parents was clamouring around them, taking photos on their phones. I was on a deadline for work and frowning at my laptop when one of the mums called out to me. 'Would you like me to get a photo of your daughter for you? I can text it to you. I can see you're busy,' she said. It was nice of her, but honestly? I wasn't going to take a photo anyway. I love my kids more than Salted Caramel Tim Tams, but I am sick of celebrating and recording every minor milestone or achievement in their lives. My daughter and her friends hadn't finished a concert; the certificates were merely for turning up and doing a term of jazz dance. And yet you'd think they were in the Bolshoi Ballet.

As I sat there feeling like the worst mum in the world, I wondered where *my* participation medal was. Where's my certificate for taking my daughter to dancing every Tuesday? For paying outrageous sums of money each term for my son to play soccer? For getting him there on time every Thursday? For reminding him to take his soccer boots? For finding those boots in the bushes by the trampoline? I reckon we should stop giving kids medals for merely turning up and give them to parents instead.

It didn't help that I had to be in three places at once that night. One kid had to be at soccer, another had to be at footy tryouts and another needed to be at jazz ballet. As always, I pulled it off – just. I called in some favours from other parents, drove like a madwoman between venues and gave the kids dinner on the run. They ate reheated burgers that tasted like seared mud flaps and made the car smell like a gymnast's armpits. And yet did they appreciate my efforts? Not really.

Don't get me wrong. I love being a mum . . . most of the time. But kids today take things for granted – particularly their parents. Often it feels like we're the ones doing the hard yards, yet they're the ones getting the reward. Schools are in on the scam, regularly throwing out a series of parental tests masquerading as fun and educational events for kids. Don't be fooled; an Easter bonnet parade is not an innocent occasion designed to celebrate the season and bring out the creativity in kids. It's a brutal battle designed to measure a parent's worth and dedication through their ability to produce a show-stopping handmade hat from recycled materials with five minutes' notice. Who makes the hat? Us. Who gets the prize for Best Hat in Show? Them. I rest my case.

It's time we came up with a whole new range of awards to be given to parents by their kids.

- Top Effort For Finding My Library Books Under My Bed Even Though I Told You I'd Already Looked There!
- Thanks a Bunch For Remembering Bastille Day and Drawing Me a Moustache With Your Favourite Eyeliner!
- You're a Hero For Remembering Footy Tryouts and Making Me Get Off the PS4 Even Though I Told You I Didn't Want To Go!
- Thanks For Helping Me Not Kill Anyone While I Was On My L-Plates!

I am kidding (sort of). I know parenthood is a reward in itself. Our kids are our medals. Their smiles are our certificates. But I wouldn't mind a trophy of my own from time to time – for achievement rather than effort.

Parents, this book is your participation medal. It's my way of saying good on you for all of the great things you do. Don't forget that no one really cares about all the things you don't do – except when you forget to take out the bin with the Christmas prawn heads in it and then go to the beach for two weeks.

Chapter 2

HYPER-PARENTING: JUST DON'T DO IT

For many parents and kids, family life is a whirlwind of obligation, guilt and competition. I get it. If I have to look at one more made-from-scratch three-tier rainbow unicorn cake on Instagram, I'll cry real unicorn tears. The Parental Stress Centre of Australia (yes, it really exists) analysed interactions with more than 186,000 parents over the past decade. It found chaotic morning routines, kids who talk back, children who never listen and tantrums from toddlers cause the most stress for parents. Sound familiar?

Parents often feel pressured and busy, even during the Covid restrictions that kept many of us home more. One survey by market research company Mumpower reflected the day-to-day frustrations of many mothers. Apart from worrying about their family's health, mums stressed about not having enough time to exercise, feeling like they were 'expected to do everything' and not having enough time in the day. Before the pandemic,

77 per cent of mums felt 'mostly positive' but this dropped to just 44 per cent after it took hold. Of course, there were upsides to stay-at-home restrictions, such as more time spent in elastic-waisted pants, more drunken Zooming and less standing in the rain watching kids lose Sunday-morning netball matches.

It's no coincidence that middle age – when most child-rearing takes place – is the least happy time for many people. The Australian Unity Wellbeing Index shows those aged 18 to 25 are the happiest, but satisfaction dips markedly during mid-life. From age 66 it starts to rise again, reaching peaks not seen since early adulthood. It's a conclusion echoed by social researcher Neer Korn, who found the least happy of all are the Gen Xers, who are in their 40s to mid-50s now, with primary- and high school-aged children. Only 59 per cent say they are satisfied, let alone happy. 'They are the middle group and they're mostly mums and dads whose lives are at the peak of stress,' Korn says. Many are also feeling the pressure of being the 'sandwich generation': stuck between raising kids and caring for ageing parents.

The Family Values report shows more than a third of adults say having children adds stress to their lives. I'd agree with this, especially when you are hurtling down the freeway late for soccer while trying to remember the team's grade and division so your ten-year-old can download the app telling you where the hell you should be going. Parents worry about lots of things: will my kids turn into nice people? Will they poo out that coin they swallowed last week for a dare? Will they ever get off Minecraft and come to dinner? It's not surprising that a survey from the

Australian National University found both men and women turned to the bottle during the initial phase of the pandemic. For dads it was to cope with the fear of job losses, and for mums it was so they could cope with the pressure of caring for kids. And I thought it was just me . . .

The Family Values report also found the greatest issue for parents is the huge amount of time kids take up. While this is true, it's got a lot to do with how hands-on parents are these days. Dr Judith Locke, a clinical psychologist specialising in parenting and child wellbeing, did some research on hyper-parenting or, as she calls it, overparenting. As she sees it, overparenting involves extreme responsiveness from the parent (i.e. extremely high levels of praise, attention and care) and low demands for the child (i.e. reduced responsibilities around the house or not implementing consequences for their child's inappropriate behaviour). She found parents who are highly responsive to their child 'may be more likely to invest intensive parental effort, and ask people and institutions the child encounters, to alter policies and procedures to maintain an ideal and pleasant life for them'.

Dr Locke says such parents want to make sure their kids' lives are 'unhindered by unpleasantness'. This may mean 'completing their homework, providing transport, helping them avoid discipline, or insisting that peers meet their child's needs'. This all takes time – a lot of time – and considerable effort. It's no wonder, she concludes, that mothers 'who attempt to increase childhood intelligence and accomplishment through intensive effort and increased time spent with children may be at risk of exhaustion, stress, anxiety, and guilt'. I conclude that they're often boring as batshit too.

Dr Locke asked 128 Australian psychologists and teachers for examples of overparenting they'd seen. Nearly one-third had seen many instances, two-thirds had seen some and only eight had not encountered any. The professionals talked about parents cutting up the food of ten-year-olds, bringing a separate plate of food for a 16-year-old to a party as he was a picky eater, carrying kids old enough to walk, stopping 17-year-olds from catching trains to school and badgering teachers about what class their child would be in, year after year. The list also includes having kids assessed for giftedness early in life, giving endless instructions such as 'don't touch that' and 'sit down', and choosing their children's friends. According to Dr Locke, the overarching principle is that, regardless of the actual level of effort, their child must be rewarded.

Such parents are also intimately involved in their children's social lives. They come to school to talk to their child's friends, confront other parents about their child missing out on party invitations and message their child's friends on social media. My daughter would never let me do the latter – no siree. She's outraged when I use abbreviations in texts like *GR8* and *BTW*, let alone take over her Instagram account.

As one professional interviewed by Dr Locke explains, 'The parents fight for the child to have what they want rather than tough it out and face the consequences.' Another says, 'I have had follow-up phone calls from parents within two minutes of a student finishing a conversation with me – wanting to express concern, frustration, about what had been discussed with their child. With the child's emotions high and a "one-eyed" view of what was discussed, they phone their parent who in turn takes immediate action to me. More often than not, their version of the "supposed" conversation is completely inaccurate.'

I can see how it happens. I know parents of high-school kids who drop off heated-up food at lunchtimes, ring or text them repeatedly during the school day and drive them around rather than let them catch public transport. (Confession: I've been guilty of all three.) It's not good for us, and it sure isn't good for the kids, who aren't allowed to grow up. My boyfriend at uni was one of these manbabies. He was 19 but his mother packed his lunch every day, with a frozen drink bottle she'd wrapped in foil and a tea towel secured with a rubber band. No wonder it didn't last with me. He could barely tie his own shoelaces, let alone conduct an adult relationship.

I am not the first person who's raised these issues. Everywhere you look, someone is having a go at parents for doing a bad job. One of the most recent is Australian author John Marsden, whose book, *The Art of Growing Up*, is a manifesto against middle-class toxic parenting. He rails at parents who view their child as their hero, think their child is extraordinary and avoid tough decisions and discipline. Throw in those who are overly controlling, too busy saving the world to care for their kids and those who want to be best pals with their children, and you've got an epidemic of poor parenting choices.

Marsden, the principal of two schools, says, 'In recent years it has become unusual for me to get an application for a Foundation enrolment from a parent who does not describe their child as gifted, imaginative and/or creative.' Marsden quotes parents who say he or she has 'taught us so much already' and who report they are 'in awe' of their offspring. These parents are not just talking their kids up to get them into Marsden's schools; it goes further than this. These kids choose their own schools, black-ban their parents' friends who don't worship them and refuse to eat sandwiches that do not have the crusts cut off. Their mums and dads compete for the title of Most Bereft Parent while they wait for their child to return home from boarding school. They also read all the books on their English lists, Marsden tells us. Sound familiar? Not to me. I am not in awe of my kids. I love them, but they are not my heroes. Half-arsed parents don't bang on like that about their kids. They let them be kids.

This all means parents are raising a generation of kidults – kids who aren't allowed to grow up, or don't want to grow up. In the major Australian cities, nearly half of all adults aged 20 to 24 are still living at home with their parents. It's partly because of soaring housing prices, but experts say it's also got a lot to do with the willingness of parents and kids to delay the seriousness of adulthood as long as possible. Dr Locke explains that when parents demand so little of kids and take so much extra responsibility for their lives, there's a reduced expectation that the child will develop maturity. This is coupled with a view that the child is a gifted genius who has special talents which need to be nurtured and admired by others. It reminds me of a four-year-old who was a designer for US clothing brand J.Crew. She and her mother made paper dresses copying famous people's outfits. Her mother put their artistic creations on Instagram where they came to the attention of J.Crew staff and were turned into clothing designs. The kid's name is Mayhem because of course it is.

Let's look in more detail at exactly what's going on with parents today. We love our kids and are happy to have them, so why are the years spent raising them so difficult?

Mums

Mother's Day rolls around every year in a blaze of advertisements telling us there's nothing more natural, eternal and spiritual than a mother's love for her children. Mothers, we're told, don't ever expect anything in return. Their love is unconditional and their devotion eternal. It's a bit over the top. I've loved just about every minute of parenthood over the past 16 years – except for the time my son spewed in my friend's hire car and she had to keep driving it for the next three days. The only eternal thing about that scenario was the smell.

But it's hard raising kids at times, and I don't just mean when your car reeks of vomit. I interviewed a group of mothers with preschool- and primary school-aged kids and they are time-poor, sleep-deprived and sick of being judged by others. They want more flexible workplaces, cheaper childcare and partners who know how to put on a load of laundry. They want others to know folding washing on the couch while watching TV is not 'me time', and they don't want to be judged if their kids have toast for three meals in a row. Mums also want to have time to look after themselves without being told by their husbands to go and have a shower because they 'deserve it'. What they *really* want is a wife to take care of them, the way they take care of everyone else. Another study of 400 mothers found two-thirds don't feel supported or understood. According to the State of Motherhood report, mums feel judged by their weight, their parenting style, their grey hair and their 'flagging career'. They feel happy spending quality time with their family and doing the things they like, which includes 'sleep, wine, hanging with friends'. They want better parental leave, superannuation reform and an end to 'mummy clichés' from brands. As one said: 'I feel like they only know beige bland perfect family mums or the crazy wine-time sort.'

There is a lot of resentment out there. In her landmark 2014 book *The Wife Drought*, journalist and broadcaster Annabel Crabb described the struggle of working women who don't have wives to look after them and their kids. As she wrote in *Good Weekend* magazine, 'women with a helpful spouse often feel like they've won the lottery, while men with a helpful spouse seem unremarkable'.

'Having it all' has become a loaded phrase that's never applied to men. Unlike most women, men get to have it all because they don't have to do it all.

Despite the heightened daily frustrations, the Covid pandemic was a reset for some. The Mumpower report made it clear mums felt a lot of pressure to be perfect before the virus hit. This meant a mum had to be 'committed to managing a household, give her children endless opportunities, hold high expectations of herself on an employment front, be a good role model, nurture relationships, be fit, well and happy'. Covid provided a brief release: 'Finally, the world stopped and enabled mums to breathe,' the report said. Marketing to Mums CEO Katrina McCarter also found that during isolation women 'relished the slower pace with no commute, school drop-offs and pick-ups and not having to live up to society's expectations of how they look'. This also meant 'less make-up, more comfortable clothes, even ditching the bra and enjoying longer sleep time'.

And yet, the demands of working from home and supervising home schooling weighed heavily on women at that time, along with fears their partners would become unemployed.

ABS figures released during the first half of 2020, when many workplaces were locked down and schools were closed, show women were three times more likely than men to be home looking after the kids fulltime – 46 per cent versus 17 per cent. Yeah, there's not a lot more time to 'breathe' when you've got to work out the difference between perpendicular and parallel lines for your grade fiver, fix the printer for your working-from-home husband and then get dinner ready before your 17-year-old orders takeaway on your credit card.

Social researcher Neer Korn agrees that mums 'still have too much on their plates and struggle to fit it all in'. All of this struggling has a darker side. The Parenting Research Centre found mums are outwardly more confident than dads – they're more likely to talk to teachers, go to parents' groups and have people to turn to for advice. But they are also more depressed and anxious, with one in three mums feeling down compared to one in five fathers.

Many women take years to come to grips with the changes in their lives once they have kids. Women often give up their own leisure time in order to fit everything in. For instance, they might love hot yoga (my friends call it fifty shades of sweat) and yet if they're a busy mum, it's the first thing to go when the going gets tough. It's because the sheer volume of things mothers do is relentless. When women become mothers, they go from spending an average of two hours a week caring for others to 51 hours a week, a 14-year study of more than 9000 Aussie households reveals. This is an extraordinary amount of time: it's almost a third of the entire week, or more than two whole days. Mums also spend more than ten hours more a week on housework, such as cooking and cleaning, than childless women. Sounds about right. Who's got time for hot yoga? The only exercise most mothers get is running late, jumping through hoops and throwing a hissy fit.

There's no doubt some days are better than others. Sometimes, I sail through the day feeling like a hero because my searing analysis about leggings not being pants became a viral hit. Other days, I flounder under the weight of multiple drop-offs and pick-ups, forgotten guitar lessons and narky teenagers who are now unfortunately taller than me. Women who work as well as raise kids often feel they can't win: they're criticised by childless colleagues for leaving on time and pitied by non-working mothers for missing out on seeing their kids fall across the finish line in the primary school cross-country marathon.

The greater amount of work done by mothers at home is balanced by a decline in women's paid work from 33 hours a week on average before motherhood, to nine hours a week after the birth. However, paid work hours increase dramatically when the children start school, peaking at 29 hours a week when the youngest is 15. Regardless of the hours of paid work women do, housework demands stay relatively constant throughout a woman's adult life, reaching 30 hours a week when children start school. That's more than four hours a day. Even after kids have left home, mothers spend 25 hours a week on housework, AIFS research shows. Yep. Aren't we massive suckers?

The global pandemic changed things for many families. The Mumpower study found two-thirds of the 820 mothers they interviewed said their relationships with their kids improved, largely thanks to the lack of external activities they had to manage. But the survey also found most mums ended up doing more, not less around the house: 57 per cent did more cooking and 46 per cent did more cleaning than before. And 46 per cent did more eating which – surprise, surprise – was not balanced by more exercise or more self-care. (As an aside, the pandemic improved the romantic relationships of 45 per cent of mums, although it didn't make any difference to their sex lives.)

AIFS director Anne Hollonds says it all 'adds up to a daunting prospect for young mothers today, who may wonder how they are going to shoulder most of the childcare and housework, while at the same time being encouraged to return to the workforce as quickly as possible,' she says. 'Not surprisingly, many mothers report feeling tired.'

Another survey of 10,000 women by Jean Hailes for Women's Health found weight management and healthy eating are the two biggest health worries of women – clearly, we're spending all our time trying to find mouthguards and ballet tights and not enough time taking the dog for a walk or eating salad. The third and fourth worries of women were mental and emotional health and anxiety, followed by menopause.

Why is caring for the people we love making us so anxious and exhausted? Is it because we're trying to do too much, not getting enough support and trying to live up to other people's expectations? It sure looks like it. It is a reflection of the intensification of mothering. American writer Judith Warner makes this point in her bestselling book *Perfect Madness*. As she said in one interview, 'One generation back, our mothers didn't put the same pressures on themselves to be sitting on the floor, building with Lego. They were ironing or gardening or cooking dinner or talking on the phone, and not feeling guilty about doing that.'

I agree. I don't remember my parents ever playing Lego with me the way I did with my kids for hour after frustrating hour when they were young. My mum may have sworn when she stepped on Lego in bare feet on the living room floor, but she would never have considered devoting her weekends to helping me and my sister make our Lego creations. Back then, Lego involved creative kid-led free play, not expensive complicated kits with page after page of word-free instructions (the worst kind). These kits are marketed to kids, but many struggle to do them alone, requiring intensive parental oversight – something half-arsed parents like me aren't that good at.

Other research by Jean Hailes for Women's Health shows one in two Australian women are worried about their weight but don't have time to cook healthy food because of work and family commitments. A lack of time is more of a barrier to healthy living than motivation or cost. Doesn't that tell you something is wrong with our lives? More than one in three women nationally can't find time to have a bubble bath or catch up with friends on a weekly basis, and 26 per cent say they have no time to themselves each month. Keeping up with demanding kids, their punishing schedules and time-intensive toys are pushing mums to breaking point. We do have enough time, but we keep on filling it with things like cooking dinner for unappreciative kids with picky eating habits rather than sharing sweat with handsome strangers at hot yoga.

While mums struggle on the home front, many find work isn't crash hot either. A survey of 800 mothers by kidspot.com.au shows nine out of ten say having kids hurts their career. Seventy-eight per cent are unhappy with their childcare arrangements and 100 per cent say they have 'conflicting' feelings about work.

Making matters worse is the gender gap which, according to the Workplace Gender Equality Agency, means women earn 14 per cent less than men for doing the same job and the same hours – that's an average of $25,000 a year less. For many women, this adds up to a million dollars less over a lifetime.

Some women suffer on the mummy track, working fewer hours than they'd like in a job they're overqualified for so they can be around to do the kids' homework and drive them to places they could walk to. Some quit paid work altogether even if they'd like to keep working. Others work more than they'd like, pretending they don't have kids in order to be taken seriously on the job. It's a case of 'Honey, I hid the kids'. If they have sick kids, they pretend it's them that's ill. Kids' school sports days? Invent a funeral (keep track of who's meant to have died). School holidays? They'll use vacation care, beg favours from other mums or send the kids on expensive camps. They do whatever they can to make it work.

It shouldn't be this hard. It doesn't have to be. We need to spend more time standing up to deadbeat bosses, reining in kids who won't do chores despite being asked a gazillion times and having nights out with friends who keep us sane. The starting point is recognising that we matter too – that our needs should be prioritised alongside everyone else's. And realising that if we don't stand up for ourselves, no one else is going to. This may mean making sure Mum's 7.30 pm hot yoga class is as much of a priority as everyone else's activities. After all, what's not to like about a form of exercise where you spend most of the time lying down and sweat from the temperature of the room rather than aerobic exertion?

Dads

Dads of my father's generation sported luxuriant moustaches, King Gee shorts and beer guts. When we were young, they'd sit us on their knees and let us 'help' them drive, sip the froth from their beer and teach us to double-dink on our bikes. Back then, dads were expected to work, hang with the kids on the weekend, watch sport on TV, burn the odd chop on a Saturday arvo and not much else. My dad wasn't all that hands-on when we were young, but he did let my sister and me plait his hair and style his biker-style sideburns.

Times have changed and many dads aren't sure what they're meant to do anymore, and I don't just mean with their facial hair. Many fathers are finding things tough, and not only because they've received another freezable beer mug for their birthday from their kids even though they don't drink beer. The biggest issue for many dads is juggling the demands of being the full-time breadwinner with wanting to be more present in their kids' lives than their own fathers were.

The three Australian dads who founded the online site The Father Hood – Luke Benedictus, Jeremy Macvean and Andrew McUtchen – reflect a new era. They all had high-profile careers in the media and marketing but found becoming dads changed them fundamentally. They didn't see why they should fit their fathering around their work. They founded The Father Hood to 'help fathers navigate through the hot mess of having kids to a place where they're living their very best lives as men'. For Macvean, becoming a dad was like entering the 'Champions League of manhood'. As he puts it, 'becoming a father is one of the greatest challenges and also opportunities a man can experience. It forces you to rethink what really matters. And there's no part of your life that is out of its reach from your career, to your relationships to the spatial dimensions of your car.'

Work is a major complication for fathers, with many employers not taking into account men's parenting needs. The gender gap in wages often means men are forced to be the full-time breadwinner. Many dads earn more than mums and their income is needed more than ever once kids arrive. Fathers also think they will be judged at work if they take the 'daddy track' – and often they are. They're sick of missing key kids' events like sports days and dance concerts but feel they'll be viewed with suspicion by their bosses if they take time off. A study by the Parenting Research Centre reveals dads are much less satisfied with the time they spend with their kids than mums. This reflects the fact that 90 per cent of fathers are employed and 92 per cent of these work full-time.

Data from the Longitudinal Study of Australian Children, analysed by researchers at the Australian National University, shows about one-third of fathers say they never, or rarely, feel work and family is in balance. This is an ongoing or persistent problem for 14 per cent of fathers. 'Fathers say they can't get to things like family events. Even when they are spending time with family they say they can't enjoy it because they're always thinking about work,' ANU researcher Dr Liana Leach says. This leads to 'fatigue, distress or emotional withdrawal as parents forgo family events or valued time with their children for work-related opportunities and expectations'. As Dr Leach explains, 'the problem is compounded for fathers who want to be with their families more but end up working 40 to 60 hours a week.'

Although more workplaces now offer parental leave and encourage dads to work part-time, few fathers do so, even if they'd like to. They feel they'll be judged as less serious workers if they go on the daddy track and will miss out on opportunities and promotions. One fascinating study from the University of Western Sydney shows dads who want to stay at home with their kids are criticised most by their own fathers, who held traditional breadwinner roles. Perhaps this is why ABS data shows men take only five per cent of primary parental leave.

There's speculation that men may have more opportunity to work more flexibly in a post-Covid world. Research from the Centre for Future Work shows 36 per cent of women and 27 per cent of men could work from home, and more are expected to do so from 2020 onwards. But this may take some years to happen. At this stage many men are stuck in the office – and stuck in the car getting there and back.

Ask most dads and they'll tell you the time they spend in the car adds significantly to their daily load. While hyper-parenting is causing Australian mums to spend one hour and twenty minutes in the car ferrying kids around every day, dads spend the same amount of time getting to and from work. That's a lot of time cooped up listening to radio shock jocks or bogan rock on Spotify. Professor Lyn Craig from the University of Melbourne compared the driving done by more than 14,000 men and women from Australia, the UK, Spain and Finland. She found men in the UK and Australia drive twice as often for work compared to women, and women drive twice as much for household-related and parenting reasons compared to men. 'There is little evidence of couples sharing the pick-up and ferrying duties at the end of the day, and across the board simultaneous or shared travel is relatively low,' Professor Craig says.

The Parenting Research Centre study also found many fathers wanted to be closer to their kids. Although some dads might spend less time than mums arguing and yelling at their children, on the flip side they might also spend less time talking with them about their day, their friends and the name of their secret crush. Perhaps it's a throwback to our fathers' generation. Many men of my father's age weren't great talkers when their kids were young: they showed their love in other ways. Their clothes were embarrassing, their little habits were annoying and many ran a mile from having to display emotion. But their actions spoke louder than words. My dad was often gruff and grumpy, but it was all a big act. When my sister and I were younger, we'd ask him for money just about every time we went out. 'Bring me the change,' he'd say sternly, handing over a tenner. 'That's a loan, you know.' 'Yes, yes,' we'd reply, always knowing we'd never be asked to repay a cent.

The Father Hood guys have edited a book called *The Father Hood*, where a range of famous men such as David Beckham, Hugh Jackman, Mark Wahlberg and Ben Stiller talk about how hard they are trying to be good fathers. I'd suggest many dads want more time with their kids, but not all of them want to be involved in the day-to-day minutiae of their children's lives. They want to do more, but on their terms. They want to be fun dads when they've got time, but don't always want to manage the household. They may love pushing kids on the swings at the park after work but don't want to sit cross-legged on the home corner mat being fed pretend cups of tea during preschool duty. Or fill out 15-page camp medical forms. Or spend three hours on the phone getting the wi-fi working again. Or move three kids' orthodontist appointments because they've worked out they'll be away when they've been booked in.

There's no glory in any of these mundane parenting tasks, but they need to be done regardless. This means women often end up doing the thankless and boring parts of parenting. Meanwhile, dads who pick their kids up a few days a week from childcare or hang out the washing without being asked are treated like heroes. It's great they're much more hands-on than their own fathers, but there's rarely an equal division of work and childcare.

A considerable amount of research backs up the unequal division of household chores, showing that men in general also do less housework than women. The greater amount of outdoor work they do – like gardening – doesn't make up for it. Even when mums pick up more hours at work, dads don't always pick up the slack at home. Sorry dads, but that's the reality. Australian Institute of Family Studies data shows the four per cent of dads who stay at home don't do as much hands-on childcare and cleaning as the 31 per cent of mums who stay home too. The study shows stay-at-home fathers do 28 hours of housework a week, 19 hours of childcare and work for four hours, a total of 51 hours. In comparison, stay-at-home mothers do 37 hours of housework, 37 hours of childcare and work for one hour; a total of 75 hours. Some of this difference reflects the fact that children with stay-at-home mums tend to be younger and need more care. But no wonder neither parent feels like they are kicking goals, even when they're literally out there on the oval at 6 pm kicking goals – or trying to.

Not all families are like this. There is an increasing number of dads who spend Saturday afternoons mulling over the sugar content of muesli in the supermarket aisle, arranging play dates and planting seedlings with toddlers without anyone asking them to. Of course, fathers who are solo dads or those who are separated have no choice but to do it all without any reward or kudos.

Despite this, there is still a tendency for dads to be seen as the second-tier parent, or in some cases, complete idiots. This attitude is not only holding them back but stopping things from being more equal on the home front. Psychologist Judith Warner says husbands can be 'shunted off to the side and made to feel like impediments to the smoothly functioning household' by the women of the family.

As Andrew McUtchen explains, 'There is not one modern dad in pop culture that we think is representative of our lives: Homer Simpson, Phil Dunphy, Daddy Pig, it's all bad. And that's why we exist. To showcase men not as loveable losers – couch potatoes, saps, buffoons – but as fathers living their best lives.' He's right. (Well, except for Bandit Heeler from Bluey, an Australian cartoon.

You know how rare positive fathering role models are when everyone's going crazy over a cartoon dog.) More often men are portrayed in TV ads as well-meaning but dumb, bumbling their way through a range of social situations and parenting challenges with charm and ineptitude. Watch him make a robot out of a panty shield in a bid to impress his kids! See him battle to work the dishwasher! Laugh as he struggles to understand what makes the air freshener dispenser randomly squirt! While TV mums are competent and can often be seen enjoying a cuppa after completing the household chores, 'Ad Dad' can barely be trusted to get the kids dressed for school in clothes worn the right way up. We'd never treat mums like this, so why is it okay for dads?

Men can also be prohibited from doing ordinary things mothers do every day, like taking their kids to the loo in a shopping centre, snapping their photo at the beach or going backstage at a ballet concert. One Melbourne man was called a 'sex offender' and a 'paedo' for taking a photo in front of a Darth Vader Star Wars display in a suburban Target store. The fact that he was only taking a selfie to send to his kids as a daggy dad joke didn't stop shoppers getting alarmed and reporting him to police because they thought he was taking photos of their child. What is modern parenting coming to when the starting point is that every father is a paedophile-in-waiting?

Sadly, outdated portrayals of men continue to flourish. Gina Ford, a well-known parenting expert, wrote in *The Contented Mother's Guide* published in 2012 that new dads need to be indulged, flattered and trained into helping with their new babies.

As she puts it, new fathers 'may feel left out and almost jealous'. And they want sex all the time. Ford talks about including 'lots of foreplay and wine' to help mums have the duty root their man will expect soon after the baby is born. 'Grin and bear it,' Ford suggests in the book. Ouch. This reflects the way too many people think about new dads: they're there to annoy us with their manly urges and are totally hopeless at looking after the baby. Why do we expect little from men, then get mad when they live down to our expectations?

A key part of half-arsed parenting involves valuing and supporting dads as well as mums. A lot of fathers would like to be a bit more hands-on around the house but feel it's not all that welcome. This is because the domestic sphere is often the woman's domain. Relinquishing power and control on the home front can be hard for some women. (Not me, I should say.) Some feel their partners won't do a good enough job while others find it easier to do things themselves because then it's done their way. Neer Korn says, 'Mums know they have to let go and be aware that their husbands might not do the job in the way they do.' He says women find it very 'liberating' to let go when they finally do so. Keen to play their part in the household, most men rise to the occasion.

Half-arsed parenting is the answer to getting the balance right. We need to be less like Queen – under pressure – and more like Frankie Goes to Hollywood – and relax. At the very least we should let dads do more, mums do less and let the kids build their own Lego battleships.

Chapter 3

MEET TODAY'S ENTITLED BRATS

You might think stressed, over-worked, time-poor parents are too busy climbing the corporate ladder and impressing others with their baking skills to pay enough attention to their kids. It's the exact opposite. These days, many mums and dads are highly committed workers with long commutes and busy schedules. But this is often coupled – out of guilt – with higher than ever expectations of them as parents. Mums and dads think they should work hard, but also be very involved at school, preschool and childcare, and hands-on at all times when they're with their kids. When they don't have time to manage this, they end up being indulgent and permissive to make up for their perceived parental failings.

This means we're facing an entitlement epidemic, thanks to a generation of children who don't hear the word 'no' often enough. The term was coined by US parenting coach Amy McCready, author of *The Me, Me, Me Epidemic*. McCready says that when 'helping and allowing becomes a way of life, we're walking the slippery slope of the entitlement epidemic'. I am sure you've all seen signs of the entitled generation at work. The family that has to leave somewhere because one child has had enough. Parents leaving work to take forgotten sport uniforms and lunchboxes to their kid's school. The parent who thinks nothing of stopping an adult conversation to let a child talk.

I was chatting with a school mum recently who told me both her children were upset when they discovered there were no snacks at home. The kids are ten and 13 and were irate when she told them there was only boring old fruit to eat after school rather than special treats, so they hung up the phone on her. What did she do about it? Probably nothing. An older lady I work with told me about her eight-year-old grandson who didn't want her to buy him any clothes anymore because they weren't 'cool enough'. Buying Spiderman and other superhero T-shirts gave her a lot of pleasure, but her grandson cried all the way home when he was forced to wear one in public. Stories like this are all around us. Another friend of mine said she frequently entertains ten or more of her 14-year-old's friends, and sometimes only one will say hello to her or thank her for having them over. These are kids she's known for more than a decade. 'They act as if I am not even there, even though I bring them food and towels for the pool,'she says. Entitled? Disrespectful? Disgraceful? You bet. And yet they're her children's friends, so she continues to ignore their rudeness and invite them over.

School holidays are a case in point. Kids bombard their parents every 3.2 seconds with demands for play dates, expensive outings and new computer games. Can you take us trampolining? Can you take us to the water park we saw the ad on TV for? Can we go buy the $90 NBL Xbox game? Same goes for birthday presents. The Family Values report found parents feel pressured to spend more than they'd like on presents for their own children and their children's friends. Their report says that 'most also believe gifts expected by children are becoming increasingly expensive or unrealistic and that children expect gifts which are not really fully appreciated'. This is despite parents spending an average of $185 on gifts for their child's birthday. $185! I reckon I bought my first car for less than that.

This sense of entitlement in kids is encouraged by parents who think their children are perfect, unique and amazing creatures who need to be protected, worshipped and adored. Half-arsed parents love their kids more than teenage boys love Lynx Africa body spray, but they know they're not always perfect. They know they can be little shits at times. They also have a healthy scepticism for some of their kids' claims. For instance, when their child tells them they've been bullied, they say, 'What did you do to them first?' Half-arsed parents don't think their kids tell the whole truth every single time about every damn thing.

Half-arsed parents also do their best to minimise the impact of their kids on others. I wish more parents did the same. A few years ago, I was lucky enough to go to Bali with some school mums. But after a few days, our holiday became a helliday thanks to other people's badly behaved brats polluting our picture-perfect views with their techno-coloured pool noodles, fluoro rashies and attention-seeking ways. They didn't talk; they screamed. They didn't walk; they ran. They didn't ask for something; they demanded it at the top of their lungs. The three kids, aged about three, five and seven, spent their mornings splashing, screaming, crying and playing. The rest of us tanned, paddled and got day-drunk on the sun lounges while these kiddies made their presence felt. What were their parents doing about it? Absolutely nothing.

When the parents finally turned their attention to the kiddie chaos a few metres away, it only made things worse. Rather than shut them up, they egged them on with baby talk and silly games. 'Dadda, Dadda, Dadda, DAAAAADDDDAAAA,' the three-year-old boy would scream at his father, who thought it was funny to steal his noodle and swim away. They loudly debated the big issues of the day. Should Charlotte put her head under the water? Will Sam stand still to get a new dose of sunscreen? Will Georgina share her noodle with Charlotte, who now wants the red one? Shoot me now.

I have three children of my own and understand that kids have good days and bad days. I also know parents have good days and bad days. If I'm sitting next to a screaming baby on a plane, I'm more likely to shout the mum or dad a drink rather than give them daggers. I didn't object to these three children being at this un-kid-friendly resort, but I did resent the fact that their parents didn't notice or care how noisy and annoying they were. Half-arsed parents know their job – even on the most basic level – is to parent their children and minimise the impact they're having on those around them. And to stop noodle fights when ladies on nearby lounges are nursing very, very large hangovers.

Clinical psychologists like Dr Locke say children like this raised in a selfish bubble are more likely to have a sense of entitlement, a lack of life skills and an inadequate sense of responsibility. All the noisy pool play, meal deliveries, participation medals and sparkly stars on every crappy piece of homework done by parents is creating a generation of brats who have a highly inflated sense of their self-worth. They think they rule the roost and, in many families, they do. As I explain later, it also fuels anxiety and a lack of resilience when this bubble of entitlement is burst by a world which fails to see them as the number-one superstar. Hyper-parenting flies in the face of a mountain of sound research that shows kids do best when they are given freedom and independence, which builds their self-confidence, resilience and problem-solving skills. As a bonus, it also stops them from being complete dickheads. Let's look at what all this crappy parenting is doing to our kids.

Kids are over-scheduled

Guilt also propels busy parents into maximising their children's development by submitting them to a punishing regime of organised activities. These days, three-month-old babies attend Pilates and pre-schoolers have more play dates than their parents. Making mud pies or playing with Barbies have given way to violin lessons, soccer practice, toddler gymnastics and accelerated learning classes. Psychologist Judith Warner explains many 'middle-class parents are struggling to give their children the type of childhood they enjoyed, which is why the next generation are being bred, like racehorses, to succeed'.

Data from the 2018 Longitudinal Study of Australian Children shows between 80 and 90 per cent of kids aged 6 to 11 do some form of extracurricular activity. Nearly one-third do two or more activities. It's not confined to affluent families; even those on lower incomes save to pay for classes costing more than $30 an hour. This approach – which was unheard of in the 70s and 80s – has been building over the last 20 years. Back in 2001, renowned American psychiatrist Alvin Rosenfeld wrote *The Over-Scheduled Child*. He called parenting the 'most competitive adult sport'. 'Today's children are so tightly scheduled that many have never invented a backyard game or had time to hang out with friends,' he said at the time. No one listened back then, and no one is listening now. Smaller backyards, lack of green space in cities and boring school playgrounds further reduce kids' chance to freely move and play.

A few years ago, I did a story about a nine-year-old who did ballet, played three musical instruments, took swimming classes and was a competition-standard gymnast. Her appointment diary began filling up at six months, when she began music lessons and baby gymnastics. Three nights a week, her mother drove her 45 minutes from home and then spent three hours in the car waiting for her to complete a three-hour class. It's insanity.

I can hear you thinking, so what? Harry loves his taekwondo and Scarlett adores her ballet. Fair enough. These classes are good to a point, and kids often enjoy them. But they require a parent to make them happen and are no substitute for real play. As the 2018 International Lego Play Well report notes, such 'organised fun' is not experienced as play by children. This is an important message to keep in mind when you say no to yet another basketball team or gymnastics class. Not only do you need to spend more time out of the car, but kids need organised activities balanced by time off. They need to get dirty, get bored, hang out with friends in the local park, walk to the shops with mates and explore the neighbourhood on their bikes. You know, the stuff we wanted them to be doing during lockdown instead of playing computer games for 23 hours a day. They won't get medals or participation certificates and no one will tell them what to do. It could be the best thing for them ever. I know it's not easy to let go – let alone say no – but bear in mind what all this hyper-parenting is doing to our kids.

Kids are anxious and stressed

All this pressure and scheduling makes kids stressed, with some suffering sleeplessness, facial tics, migraines and bed-wetting. Analysis of more than 15,000 paediatric consultations shows the overall proportion of Australian children who have a medical diagnosis of anxiety rose from 4.4 per cent to 7.6 per cent between 2008 and 2013. Other studies show up to 11 per cent of children are at serious risk of mental health problems such as clinical depression and anxiety. There is also an increase in the number of children being prescribed medication to help them deal with their conditions. Between 2009 and 2012, the biggest jump in anti-depressant prescriptions was for children aged 10 to 14.

Experts put the spike down to issues such as lack of sleep, excessive screen time, bullying and overscheduling of school and extracurricular activities. They say parental intrusiveness is linked to higher levels of separation anxiety in children, especially when they have to complete actions themselves. Psychologist Kirrilie Smout, whose practice in South Australia treats 250 children a week, estimates about a quarter of children are anxious in their daily lives but don't meet the threshold for a medical diagnosis. 'They continually seek reassurance, constantly question when things are happening, avoid things that make them worried and often have physical symptoms such as tummy aches, headaches and feeling panicky,' she says. These conditions are often attributed to overbearing, perfectionist parenting creating a generation of kids too scared to do things for fear of failing.

Schedule in some messy play

When I was a kid, we'd spend hours in the backyard with a hose in the dirt patch and 'bake' lots of yummy mud pies which our parents would pretend to eat, especially after they'd had a few Swan lagers. Now the only way some kids are allowed to get dirty is at an indoor play centre. One such centre in Melbourne offers 'messy play' sessions in order to meet children's sensory and tactile needs. The poor little buggers are so dirt-averse that their parents have to pay for them to have gooey, sticky, dirty fun – with aprons on, of course. It's indoors (no risk of sunburn or wandering off), paid (so parents know it will be up to scratch) and supervised (so there's no chance of them making mistakes). I think it's sad that parents have to pay to have others supervise and organise something that used to be nothing more than random good fun with the neighbourhood kids.

Messy play classes are an apt symbol of parenting today. One survey of 500 Australian families shows kids spend less than an hour a day doing things outside, but up to four hours a day indoors. The findings also show that compared to one generation ago, kids spend 30 per cent less time outside and twice as much time on screens. The Golden Circle survey also found 62 per cent of parents say they want to spend more time camping, and four in five believe being outside is good for kids. And yet we don't make this happen. Kids spend 84 per cent of their time on indoor activities.

The irony is that most parents aren't happy with the way their kids are being raised – even though they're the ones raising them. There's a massive gap between what parents say they want and what they do. A major reason for this is concern about safety. Parents want their children to get outside more, be alone with their friends and have crazy adventures like they used to as kids, but they're worried they won't be safe.

One state government study of kids aged eight to 13 found they want more freedom to explore their neighbourhoods, but are held back by parents who fear hoons, bullies, magpies, dogs, strangers, 'weirdos' and traffic risks. Such fears come from a diverse range of sources including media outlets playing up dangers to promote stories, and advertisers selling products such as GPS tracking devices for kids. It's a pity because most parents' fears are totally unfounded. Although traffic dangers are valid in busy areas, crime statistics don't support the fear of strangers. Kids are much more at risk of being harmed by a male not biologically related to them in a relationship with their mother than an unknown person on the street.

Parents also don't trust their kids to make good decisions. It's because they never get to decide anything for themselves. It's crazy. The vast majority of kids will learn good road sense and make sound choices about who they can trust only when they're out and about in their neighbourhoods. Working out when it's safe to cross a road or ask a stranger for directions teaches kids a lot about how the world works and what they're capable of. Sadly, imagining the worst has become so ingrained that it's almost impossible to overcome the biggest barrier of all – our own minds. Wrapping kids in cottonwool isn't making them safe, it's making them inactive and us paranoid.

It reminds me of New Yorker Lenore Skenazy, who's the original free-range mum. In 2008, Skenazy caused an international furore because she let her nine-year-old son ride the subway alone. She was dubbed 'America's worst mom' as a result. But do you know what? Her son was fine, as she knew he would be. And yours will be too, if you let them off the leash once in a while.

Dudes with 'tude

Psychologist Michael Carr-Gregg wrote a landmark book about girls in 2006 called *The Princess Bitchface Syndrome*, detailing a type of teenage girl who is rebellious, careless and bitchy. Smaller families mean these girls have less access to positive role models in older siblings, but also have 'time-poor parents who take the path of least resistance, avoid discipline and overindulge their daughters'. In the recent edition written with Elly Robinson, Carr-Gregg gives the example of Matilda, who breaks a curfew, hits her brother, calls her friend a 'dumb bitch', yells at her mother and then flounces off to her friend's house when she is being told off. Her mother then rings the friend's mum to hear her described as a 'very sweet girl'. She is – to everyone but her family. Matilda is the product of hyper-parenting, which results in parents losing control of their own kids because there's no respect and no boundaries.

Carr-Gregg and Robinson think parents are losing their authority and giving in to girls who are fast-tracking themselves to adulthood. They wave the white flag because they don't know how to deal with these girls, whose physical development is way ahead of their emotional progress. One common approach is for parents to want to be their teen daughter's mate, neglecting to appreciate that the last thing a 13-year-old wants is a 50-year-old best friend. In their eyes this validates their permissive choices and shows they're the adored parent they want to be. Funnily enough, their kids rarely see it this way.

Carr-Gregg and Robinson did a boys' version of the book called *The Prince Boofhead Syndrome*. They describe a subset of boys who are lazy, selfish, disrespectful, ungracious, self-absorbed and contemptuous. These boys have 'never been challenged when they refuse to take out the rubbish bins, pick up the dog poo or stack the dishwasher,' Carr-Gregg and Robinson say. And there are no consequences. Such boys 'have been brought up to see the world as one giant, personalised, all-singing, all-dancing, 24/7 catering service that operates exclusively for them'.

Mothers often cop the brunt of such behaviour, which is based in a fundamental lack of respect for women. 'I heard one boy say to his mother – who was paying his very expensive schooling – "You do not have my permission to attend any of my sporting events",' Carr-Gregg told me. The mother was flabbergasted but wasn't willing or able to object to his views. In the book, Carr-Gregg and Robinson give the example of another 13-year-old boy who called his mother a 'stupid hag' for bringing him the wrong folder at school. 'You are just bloody hopeless. Just rack off!' this boy said to his mother.

These little princes and princesses grow up with a very inflated sense of what they are going to do in life. When I was growing up in the 70s, I wanted to be a teacher or a shopkeeper and, failing that, Linda Stoner from *Cop Shop*, because she had blonde hair and carried a nice handbag. These days, kids are more obsessed with so-called fantasy professions. They want to be professional footballers, YouTubers, Apple geniuses or ballet dancers, according to research from the Australian Institute of

Family Studies. Dr Jennifer Baxter surveyed 3378 teenagers and found very few kids aged 14 and 15 want to work in less prestigious jobs such as retail, hospitality or manufacturing. This is despite the fact that these jobs make up half of the workforce. Instead, they want to be actors, TV music hosts, circus acrobats and 'Interspace Emperors'. Such occupations make up 11 per cent of desired jobs but take up 1.3 per cent of the labour market. Older kids are the same, with few wanting office, sales, managerial or trade jobs.

Even young kids are dudes with 'tude. Once upon a time, having attitude meant you were rude; now it is celebrated and encouraged. There's even a website called Vulgar Baby which sells 'Badass baby threads'. Its logo is a baby with its middle finger extended upwards. Tasteless offerings include onesies with sayings such as 'Dingo bait', 'The condom broke' and 'Party in my crib. Let's get tit-faced.' I even came across one with 'Hung like a six-year-old' written on it. Why would any parent put their baby in that? Kids sport similar grungy, punk-inspired outfits. I'm sure you've come across parents who put children as young as two in leather boots, camouflage commando pants, rock-star sunglasses and sleeve tattoo tops. Often these too-cool-for-school kiddie outfits are topped off with a large dose of surliness and a side serve of moodiness, with kids living up to the clothes their parents choose for them.

We need to change the way we're bringing up our kids. While parents are struggling, our kids are sagging under the weight of expectation, entitlement, anxiety and really bad fashion choices.

Nanna knows best

Grandparents are more involved in their grandkids' lives than ever – mostly as comfortably dressed unpaid labourers. Most don't want to be paid, but they do want to be listened to if they ever deign to offer advice about their children's parenting choices. Here's one oldie brave enough to offer his opinion on the younger generation: 'The children now love luxury; they have bad manners, contempt for authority; they show disrespect for elders and love chatter in place of exercise. Children are now tyrants, not the servants of their households. They no longer rise when elders enter the room. They contradict parents, chatter before company, gobble up dainties at the table, cross their legs, and tyrannise their teachers.' That was Socrates writing in 428 BC, but it could have been Nanna Carol after she looked after her grandkids last Wednesday.

A survey on Grannynet shows grandparents believe the old courtesies are being erased. They think parents want their kids to be 'free to express themselves' rather than reined in by old-fashioned good manners. Grandparents are frustrated by kids who don't say 'please' and 'thank you', don't use basic table manners, don't write thank-you letters and don't say 'excuse me' before interrupting. I don't blame them. Too many parents today are scared to stand up to their kids. Carr-Gregg tells this story in *Strictly Parenting*: 'I recently took a Skybus from Tullamarine into Melbourne. The bus was so crowded that I had to stand in the aisle. While I was standing there, I saw a father ask his seven-year-old son to sit on his knee so that an older passenger could take the boy's seat. "I don't want to," the boy said stubbornly. To my amazement, the father did not insist and the child had a comfortable journey while his elders pitched and reeled around him.'

One study of 1000 Australian parents found basic phrases like 'may I', 'please', 'excuse me' and 'thank you' are rarely used by children. Three out of four parents think children are less well-mannered than in previous generations, and want teachers to help them impart basic courtesy to their kids. It also found 91 per cent of parents want values and manners taught in schools. This is part of the problem: parents are outsourcing their role in the mistaken belief that it's other people's jobs to perform the hard parts of raising their kids.

Like most parents, I find myself bleating reminders about good manners until I am blue in the face. Mealtimes are an opportunity for bad behaviour to come to the fore. 'Sit up straight don't eat with your hands don't eat off your knife take your plate out say thank you eat your vegetables don't feed the dog your peas put your knees down,' I repeat ad nauseum every time we all sit down to eat. It's bloody exhausting. This is why we should listen to grandparents when they offer advice about our kids' behaviour and manners. Who knows when we might need them to pop over and give us a break for a year or twenty?

Consider the consequences . . . of not saying no

A few years ago, a movie called *Parental Guidance* spoofed modern parenting. Actor Marisa Tomei played a mum who was leaving her kids with her parents, played by Billy Crystal and Bette Midler.

'There's a way we talk to our kids,' she told them. 'Where you would say "no", we say "maybe you should try this".

'You would say, "don't", we say, "consider the consequences".

'You would say "quit your whining, you're giving me a headache", we would say "use your words".'

Sadly, this molly-coddling approach isn't confined to Hollywood. In *The Strength Switch*, University of Melbourne psychologist Lea Waters says parents should focus more on what children do well, and the positive character traits they have. For example, instead of saying 'stop fighting', say 'Hey, how about some co-operation here?' I agree parents should be positive in general, but why protect kids' precious feelings while telling them off? Why can't parents say Stop? Or No? Or Don't?

Another guide to complimenting kids by counselling psycho-therapist Katherine Phillip says mums and dads should stop using terms like 'good girl', 'well done' and 'you're so clever'. Much better, in her view, is 'you did it!' Even calling a child 'cute' or 'handsome' is a no-no because it 'can lead to body image issues expecting to fulfil that image always,' says Phillip. Instead, we are to focus on their smiles or clothes. Again, I agree too much focus on looks and body shape can lead to image issues, but, honestly, what's wrong with saying 'good girl'? Or 'well done'?

Teachers and childcare workers are told to take a similar tack. In one Australian state government guide, an early childhood teacher reconsiders asking a slow-eating child to hurry up and finish morning tea for fear of bullying him. Again, I'm left wondering who's in charge. Not the teachers or parents, it seems. Half-arsed parents don't have time for such nonsense. When parents need a guide to giving compliments, it's a sure-fire sign that things are out of whack.

I'm left sympathising with Artie, Billy Crystal's character, who couldn't cope with his daughter's idea of turning everything into 'teachable moments'. 'All I hear is "Use your words. Use your words", but the word they never use with the kids is "No!"' he says.

He's right.

Kids now don't get told no. Or be quiet. Do what you are told. Stop talking. Parents end up tip-toeing around their kids, too scared to tell them off for fear of making them anxious or violating their human rights as autonomous individuals. Half-arsed parents think kids need to be encouraged and supported, but they also need to know who's boss. Us – not them. Parents need to take back control. Our kids need to realise we're not just there to meet their needs, pay for things and deliver correctly worded compliments. It's time for parents to rebel. As we'll see, a key part of being a half-arsed parent is knowing there's a time to be good, a time to be embarrassing and a time to be plain bad.

Chapter 4

WHEN GOOD MUMS GO BAD

We know parenting is the toughest gig there is. It doesn't take mums and dads long to find they will never again go to the toilet alone, sleep through the night, or get laid without a horrified pre-schooler standing in the doorway exclaiming, 'What's Mummy doing to Daddy?' Getting anywhere via car involves suffering through *Frozen* on endless loop or listening to your teenager cheer as she obliterates third-world nations while playing *Infection*. (It's a video game where you win when you've wiped out the human race with a unique virus that can't be cured with antibiotics. It's what passed as fun before the Covid pandemic hit.) The half-arsed way is to stop trying to impress others and get on with enjoying parenthood again. A big part of this is caring less what others think, having fun on your own terms (and not just when it suits the kids) and being bad now and then instead of good all the time. Who knows? When you're worrying less, you might even have a bit of fun and enjoy the occasional Saturday morning bonk without an audience.

In the past few years, there's been a rise in the number of books, TV shows and movies about parents who go rogue because they're fed up with the pressures of parenting. This book fits squarely in this genre, and I am proud of the inglorious trail of imperfect parents who have come before me.

Trisha Ashworth and Amy Nobile are the authors of *I Was a Really Good Mom Before I Had Kids.* They're early pioneers of the Bad Mum genre. The book was given to me in 2008 by my oldest friend Edwina, presumably because it reminded her of me. Ashworth and Nobile throw away their kids' drawings when they're sleeping, look forward to going to work and wish they had their own adults-only apartments. They love their kids but sometimes they look at their mummy lives and think, 'I can't believe I gave up nine months of drinking for this'.

Coming back to the book a decade later, I found handwritten notes in the back suggesting it was revelatory when I first read it. *I only work two days a week but sometimes give my kids McDonald's or macaroni and cheese, not vegetables*, I wrote. That was only the tip of the iceberg. *I snap at the kids at the end of a bad day at work. I can't be casually, effortlessly stylish. I don't earn enough money. I spend too much on food. I take a magazine to the park instead of watching the kids. I should make the kids (then aged 3 and 5) do more but it's easier to do it myself.* And my favourite: *I give my daughter a cuddle instead of a new nappy at night because I am too tired to get out of bed sometimes.* Most of these things I can't even remember, but they feel true.

Sh*tty mums

Another of the early books was *Sh*tty Mum*, written by a group of UK mothers back in 2012. Its authors make a commitment to 'parenting with 40 per cent effort'. The book was designed to be skimmed while mums were hiding out in the loo, escaping their children. Chapters include 'How to tell if your friends are only pretending to like your baby's name', 'How to leave your child in the car while you dash into 7-Eleven' and 'It's come to your attention that your child is merely average'. And my favourite: 'Stop not taking the easy way out.'

As the *Sh*tty Mum* authors – Mary Ann Zoellner, Alicia Ybarbo, Karen Moline and Laurie Kilmartin – see it, children and babies are 'selfish and suicidal'. 'They want everything you have and they want it now. They don't care about ruining your abs or killing your sex life and they sure as hell don't give a shit that you only slept four hours last night. Kids – and their proto-versions, babies – don't care about the mortgage, saving for retirement, or the way they add six inches to the lengths of your breasts. They want you to quit your job and pay more attention to them.'

Ain't that the truth. Sh*tty mums work hard to even the playing field. They let the kids wee on the side of the road rather than finding petrol stations. And they text their friends instead of pushing their kid on the swing for hours. That's the half-arsed way. I hail from the same 'she'll be right' school of raising kids, which puts parents in control and makes sure kids don't win all the time. Occasionally, my kids even get lucky enough to use public toilets instead of the bushes. It's not so much a case of 'I don't know how she does it', but 'I don't know why she bothers' and 'Eeww, I wish she hadn't done that'.

I've been heading into sh*tty mum territory for years now. As a half-arsed parent, it's okay to admit this. In fact, people like you more once you do. I once left my daughter at crèche when she was a few weeks old. I didn't forget her for a few minutes; I forgot she existed and drove all the way home without her. When he was a toddler, I once gave my older son my car keys to play with and he used them to lock himself in the car. It was not my proudest parenting moment. I was hysterical – he was calm. I've also lost my younger son in Target countless times. Be sympathetic next time you see someone with a snot-streaked face zig-zagging down the aisles crying frantically and calling out loudly. It's not my son – it's me looking for him.

As time goes on, my standards are slipping lower. I give things in the fridge the sniff test rather than abide by use-by dates. I once gave my kids stale sandwiches for lunch as I'd been out with the girls the night before and skipped the supermarket shopping. And don't get me started on my car: I only cleaned it this week because someone drew a penis in the dust on the rear windscreen.

No doubt you've got a few parenting fails up your sleeve too. I once put a call-out on Facebook and was inundated with similar stories. One pal detailed the time she ignored her toddler wanting to go to the toilet, only to find him, minutes later, weeing onto the baby who was sleeping beneath him in the double-decker pram.

Another sent her son to school with a panty shield stuck to the back of his jumper from the dryer because she was late and didn't notice until he walked into the playground. And another said her third child's first proper word was the c-word. True story. He learnt it from her.

This is why half-arsed parents need a dose of sh*tty mum and dad every now and then. We don't want to be bad parents, but we shouldn't have to be perfect either. One study from the UK shows confessions of our failings as mothers have 'transformative and therapeutic' impacts on other mums, especially those who are facing stigmatised conditions such as post-natal depression. It's also great for building kids' resilience and showing them they're not the only ones who matter. The ultimate sh*tty mum, TV's Roseanne, once said, 'If the kids are still alive at the end of the day, I've done my job.'

Bad Moms

A few years ago, the half-arsed parenting movement received a further boost thanks to the US movie *Bad Moms*. Bad moms fantasise about having an accident so they can spend two weeks alone in hospital. They'd rather go to Afghanistan than watch another kids' sporting match. And they skip work to get day-drunk with the girls at the movies. *Bad Moms* stars my ultimate girl crush Mila Kunis as Amy, a dysfunctional workaholic with a slacker boss, a deadbeat husband and demanding kids. When Amy's daughter says she's going to be late for her first soccer practice, Amy replies:

'I'm sorry, you know I am trying hard.' 'That's what makes it so sad. Try harder,' is the comeback from her daughter.

Amy and her friends Kiki and Carla, played by Kristen Bell and Kathryn Hahn, go bad after too many run-ins with bratty kids, mean girls and emergency parents' association meetings. A Power-Point presentation detailing prohibited ingredients for a cake stall makes Amy see red. 'No BPA, no MSG, no BHA, no BHT, no sesame, no soy and, of course, no nuts or eggs or milk or butter or salt or sugar or wheat,' reads out Queen Bee mean mum Gwendolyn, played by Christina Applegate. Amy realises she's had enough with competitive mothering, where women are judged by their willingness to slave over homemade baked goods after doing a full day's work. 'I'm done,' she announces.

Actor Rachel Griffiths found the same thing, telling one interviewer that she encountered American women who would 'stay up all night baking cupcakes for their kids' bake sales when they're a lawyer working an 80-hour work week, just to prove they're a good mommy'. Griffiths didn't think this applied to Aussie mums. 'You just stop at the 7-Eleven and buy the cupcakes. And no one would judge you for it,' she says.

I don't think the pressure here is as intense, but it's definitely there. The rules for the cake stall at my son's preschool ran to four pages, and the list of banned ingredients was longer than my arm. Even allowing for allergies, that's ridiculous. Every family was expected to bake something from scratch, with shop-bought items specifically outlawed. I was scared we'd be searched at the gate for packaged labelling to pick up non-baking cheaters.

The movie was a breakthrough moment for me. I even organised a *Bad Moms* movie night with some mum friends. We drank a truckload of champagne in a local bar and then staggered next door to watch the movie. One of the mums I went with is a high-level administrator and a single mum tired of being judged by 'smug marrieds' – as Bridget Jones called them. My friend is sick of being made to feel guilty for spending her weekends with her son instead of doing working bees in the schoolyard. She laughed so much during the movie that she snorted champagne out of her nose.

Another woman who came is a lawyer who's sick of being work-shamed by non-working mums. She's not even 40, but already feels her life is an endless grind of guilt. 'A guy who started with the firm three years before me is now my boss,' she told us that night. 'And mums at school keep asking me when I'll be able to make it to our sons' soccer game, which is at four-thirty on a Friday. Four-thirty! Doesn't anyone work anymore?' Schools don't think so, often scheduling concerts and events when parents are busy earning a living to pay for their kids' schooling. Ironic, isn't it? Stay-at-home mums don't have it much better, as they're often taken for granted by working parents who assume they're going to volunteer for everything at the school and drive everyone's kids around. Parents often can't win regardless of what they do.

The *Bad Moms* night was a brilliant reminder that mums should stop trying to be so damned perfect all the time and have a bit more fun. It'd been a long time since I was shitfaced before 9 pm on a school night. The next day, I struggled. The kids had

Twisties and dip-it biscuits for lunch (which they had to get themselves because I didn't get up in time). I forgot my daughter needed to dress up for a convict excursion and didn't fill in the forms for the museum trip. I also skipped a work meeting and had a late-morning latte by myself instead. If I could have engineered an accident and a hospital stay, I would have.

Having fun isn't always easy, but it's always worth it in the long run. Everyone needs to be a bad parent from time to time. It's the best fun you'll have with your clothes on, trust me.

Real mums

Sometimes bad mums go by the more respectable name of real mums. A few years ago I came across a proud real mum called Amanda Cox, who was known as Mad Cow by her many online followers. Amanda wanted women to 'fess up to their mummy misdemeanours' rather than beat themselves up about them. 'We look for stories that are very real, although often not spoken aloud and make the rest of us feel "normal",' she said. 'We are not aiming to glorify or encourage "bad" behaviour of mums, but rather to normalise the day-to-day misgivings and mistakes every mum makes.' Finalists included Chantal, whose five-year-old daughter wasn't allowed out of bed until 7 am. Chantal once 'purposely put the clock in her room back 30 minutes so we could have a sleep in'. Chrystal was a finalist for admitting she has chucked out more than one pair of her son's undies rather than washing them. Katrina, who had children aged two and four and worked at home, answered the phone while on the toilet. She was in the middle of a conversation with a potential customer when her four-year-old boy shouted, 'Mum you forgot to pull your pants up, your bum's hanging out'.

This sort of thing happens to many parents (like me) who have the poor judgment to combine pre-schoolers, a home office and paid employment. Katrina's mummy motto was, 'keep laughing at least 70 per cent of the time otherwise you will go stir-crazy'. Jodi, another finalist, once pulled a sickie from reading duty at school, saying, 'I don't want to talk to my own children, let alone 41 others'. Right on, sister. The difference is that instead of curling up in shame, half-arsed parents laugh about the times they are less than perfect. Let's face it, that's a lot of the time.

These days, hyper-parenting is so pervasive that it doesn't take much for real mums or dads to stand out. One Sydney mum, Carly Hall, got a shout-out for posting a photo on a Facebook mums' group showing her kids' day off. She slept in and couldn't get her seven-year-old ready for school, so she had a day at home. She then took her daughter and the three younger siblings to a café. The older two had Slurpees while the younger two slept in the pram 'just so I could have a coffee in peace (on a separate table) and scroll through Facebook while ignoring them'. Onya Carly. Sounds very half-arsed to me.

Another real-life wonder is Mamamia.com.au writer Holly Wainwright, who wrote a story recently about her 'I don't list'. Wainwright details the 'peak parenting' problem that heaps pressure and expectation on women. 'Are you there, smiling, at the school gate daily, after fitting in every important meeting and not missing an email?' Wainwright asks.

Her conclusion is that women need to hear what other women aren't doing, not how women 'do it all'. Her 'I don't list' includes not making birthday cakes, not making her daughter practise her violin, not exercising, not decorating, not entertaining and not volunteering at her child's school. This means she has time for 'lying on the couch under a blanket watching *Australia's Got Talent* and eating biscuits'.

Aaah, this is one top half-arsed chick. Kudos to you, Wainwright. I also don't do many of those things. This year, I stopped making my 11-year-old practise his guitar. It was only ten minutes or so a day, but I always had to make him do it and he always wanted me to pick the songs and sit there and listen to him. So, one day, I stopped making him do it and now he never gets out the guitar between his weekly lessons. Do you know what? Nobody's even noticed. His teacher hasn't complained, my son hasn't asked why I've stopped forcing him to play and everyone's a whole lot happier.

Another real parenting superstar is Kristy Vallely, who blogs as 'The Imperfect Mum'. I interviewed her a few years ago. I wrote: 'Last week she dropped her kids to school wearing her pyjamas, and she isn't afraid who knows it. Her bedroom sports a "floordrobe", her garden is filled with weeds and she's got about 3000 loads of washing to do.' As Vallely sees it, 'perfection does not exist – yet as mothers so many of us are all striving for it.'

'The moral of the story is don't compare because you will just be comparing yourself to something that doesn't exist. Life isn't a highlight reel, it's *all* the bits in between,' she says. 'We're not seeing the sink over-flowing with dishes. We're not seeing the fights they have with their husband. We're not seeing the mounting laundry. And we're not seeing the dirty and sticky floors.'

A checklist from Vallely for other imperfect mums includes taking her kids to school or preschool on a pupil-free day, taking kids to school wearing fancy dress a week early, and forgetting to take kids to birthday parties. Your honour, I plead guilty on all three counts. Remember the feeling of joy that comes with finding a park out the front of the preschool giving way to dread and then horror when you find out no one else is there because preschool's not on? Or that text from another mum wondering why your child didn't come to the party you forgot about? *Hope you're okay – I know how much Ethan was looking forward to the party*. And don't get me started on fancy dress. There's a reason why my kids take any dress-ups with them in their school bag rather than wear them to school – maybe I've got the right day, maybe I haven't.

I am not surprised that 40 per cent of mums aspire to be perfect although only three per cent rate themselves as such, according to one survey. What an astonishing gulf between aspiration and reality. It says one in five mums tells white lies to impress other mums, although many are happy to 'muddle through and even revel in their imperfections'. The same data shows half of all mums admit to giving their kids lollies before bed, letting them go longer than they should without baths or showers and 'losing it' in public places such as playgrounds and supermarkets. They've even served them food dropped on the floor. Sites like kidspot.com.au are packed with great stories from mums admitting all the ways they fall down. Writer Lucy Kippist does a 'happy dance' when she gets to work and escapes her kids, doesn't move until she hears the third 'Mummy!' in the middle of the night and does not do nit treatments every time a note comes home from school.

Hooray for these half-arsed parents! I'm not saying parents should act like this all the time, but we should accept that perfection is neither possible nor desirable.

Detached dads

Funnily enough, the Bad Dads movement has yet to take off. No doubt many of these sentiments apply equally to fathers, but dads appear unwilling to showcase their failings to a national audience. And yet there are a few 'bad dads' around. One is US father and *Roads & Kingdoms* podcaster Nathan Thornburgh, who wrote an article in *Time* magazine called 'The Detached Dad's Manifesto: How fathers can contribute by just chilling out'. Thornburgh rails against overbearing hyper-controlling mothering that dictates women watch their diets while pregnant in order to 'ward off suboptimal fetal intelligence' and feel they need to 'suffer authentically during natural childbirth'. (For the record, half-arsed parents will never sign up to either of those things.)

Thornburgh writes, 'If a mother's instinct often pushes toward more protection, a father's instinct tends to be that the kid is going to be just fine ... Call it detachment fathering. This can mean many things. It's not feeling a twinge of guilt if you don't want to splurge on organic vegetables. It's letting your kid watch a cartoon if you're too tired or busy to dive into a more enriching activity. Again, without guilt, because you know the kid has the important things – love, food, shelter – and that his intellectual diet can slack from time to time.' Of course, detachment parents are not so distant that they will go out for milk and never come back. 'But a little dose of fatherly distance from the expectations set by everyone from William Sears to your peers in mommy-and-me yoga can be just what the doctor ordered,' Thornburgh says. Sounds good to me.

A book called *Mommy Guilt* by Julie Bort, Aviva Pflock and Devra Renner says twice as many dads as mums feel no parental guilt at all. Dads who feel guilty worry about concrete things, like school grades or the way kids eat. Mothers, on the other hand, feel guilty about all sorts of impossible things to measure or control, like their kids' emotional state. Half-arsed parents will follow the detached dad's lead and stop letting other people guilt us into feeling bad about the things we're not doing well. Remember, if they were that important, we'd care enough to put in more effort in the first place.

Embarrassing parents

Embracing your inner badness has a nifty spin-off. It's embarrassing for the children. Half-arsed parents sometimes go out of their way to be silly or naughty because they love watching their kids squirm. Not only does it put those nasty pint-sized rodents in their place, but it reminds them we're people too, and not just parents. Embarrassing my kids is something I've elevated to an artform. I once took my clothes off for the newspaper to make a statement about body image, went pole dancing for a story and got roasted at a kids' junior footy function for something I'd written about a footy dad. Whoops . . .

These days, my kids are older and it doesn't take much to make them embarrassed. Talking with my friends about bikini waxing, how hot our first boyfriends were and the tattoos we wanted to get will do it. (Or maybe it was how hot the bikini wax was and the boyfriends we wanted to get?)

When my kids need taking down a peg or two, I reminisce loudly about their younger years. 'Remember the time you painted with your own poo in the cot when your grandfather was baby-sitting?' 'Remember that stage you went through where you would randomly touch strange women in the street as you walked past them?'

Aaah, good times.

Kissing them at the school gate, using their pet names in front of their friends and taking selfies in public places are other sure-fire embarrassment triggers. Head to the internet and there are many examples of parents using social media to shame their offspring. One mother wrote on her son's Facebook wall, 'He's not "a gangsta" who will "whip a ho's ass". He is a 15-year-old who was afraid of the dark until he was 12 and cried at the end of *Marley and Me*.' The internet is full of photos of parents celebrating their child's conception dates on their kid's social media pages and posting hints about why it's best to buy top-quality condoms.

My favourite is this mum.

Kid's post: 'Nothing is really lost until your mom can't find it.'

Friend asks: 'What about your virginity?'

His mum then replied: 'It's in his bedroom . . . under a pile of dirty socks.'

I also love the idea of Madonna's daughter Lourdes struggling with her mother's 2011 *Vanity Fair* Oscars party outfit. Behind every famous mum hamming it up for the cameras in a black lace leotard, there's a teenager saying, 'Mum, do you *have* to wear that?'. Same goes for Lionel Ritchie, whose daughter Nicole revealed she and her sister used to say to each other, 'Someone tell him to stop dancing'. My daughter tells me I'm embarrassing when I scream out her name in public, dance and lick my fingers to wipe food off her face.

Half-arsed parents approve of such shenanigans. Most times, embarrassing our kids is so easy we do it without even trying. This happened a year or two ago when I took a friend's daughter to buy a strapless bra to wear at her 18th birthday party. She needed a bra that stayed up while she was dancing so I made her dance-walk through the bra shop to road-test each one. (She had clothes on over the top, in case you were wondering.) It was pretty funny. Or so I thought. My son's friends were laughing when I told them about it later that day on the way to their basketball game. I even did some pretty cool dance moves with my arms at the traffic lights. But when the other kids got out, I was met with a glare from my then-14-year-old son. 'Mum, I can't believe you told that story about bras. You must never tell that story again,' he said. 'In fact, if you could never talk to my friends again, that would be great.' (Note that I was not allowed to talk to his friends, but I was still allowed to drive them places.)

Hooray for embarrassing parents. There's a certain satisfaction to be had from making our kids mad. I'm pretty sure my parents didn't spend their time seeking my approval. They didn't care what I thought until I was old enough to drive and thus be useful to them. And yet kids today think it's okay to boss their parents around. My own kids are always ready to step in to tell me when I'm crossing the line. You are not cool. You are not hip. Please do not try to be, they tell me. Don't dance. Don't sing. Don't tell jokes because they're not funny.

I'm not allowed to kiss them in front of their friends, cheer too loudly at sporting matches or use spit to make their hair sit down at the school gates. I am not allowed to ask my son if he's got a girlfriend and I am not allowed to suggest any of my friends' daughters as potential dates. I am not allowed to mention any of the following in front of my son's friends: body odour, armpits, body hair or the fact that he had a can of Lynx Seduction confiscated at the airport recently. I am not allowed to use any 'young-person words', like 'lit', 'mint' or 'fleek' – especially incorrectly. For your information, 'fleek' means cool. And it's 'on fleek'. As in 'your eyebrows are on fleek'. (My daughter told me that.)

What my kids don't realise is that I have an endless supply of stories about sex, bras, puberty, flirting, periods and all the other things they find embarrassing. The more they protest, the more likely I am to roll them out. I am a half-arsed parent, hear me roar. If my son doesn't behave, I am going to tell his friends more bra stories, like the one about when I first wore a bra to a school disco. It came undone and I couldn't do it back up so took it off and hid it in the toilets. A teacher found it and held it up in front of everyone as evidence girls were 'getting fresh' with the opposite sex. A friend piped up and said to me loudly in front of everyone, 'Isn't that yours?'. Of course, the only thing more embarrassing than telling stories about bras is writing stories about bras in a book. Sorry, honey. It had to be done. Be nicer to your mother next time.

Half-arsed parents are people too, and need to go rogue once in a while. And, in some cases, several times a week. But please remember that a bit of bad parenting can backfire. One Mother's Day, my younger son gave me a card he made at school with a photo of me trying to look sexy while dancing on a pole for that work assignment. He found the photo of me in stripper heels, clinging onto the pole like it was a giant dildo between my legs, on Google Images. His prep teacher helped him print it out and my son glued it onto the card, pleased as punch. On fleek? You bet.

Chapter 5

THE SCARY NEW WORLD OF PARENTING

In all the years my children have been at childcare, kindergarten and primary school, I have seen many changes in the way kids are treated and educated which make it harder for half-arsed parents. Things we've enjoyed for decades have been declared suspect and have been banned, made-over or sanitised. Some of it is due to the rise of extreme forms of political correctness, which rebadges speech and actions that have been acceptable for generations as offensive. Once, kids were left to recite the rhymes, read the books and play with the toys of their choice. Now, adults step in to make sure toys are gender neutral, rhymes aren't scary and books are updated.

For many years at preschools, three and four-year-olds would have an Easter egg hunt, hold a nativity play and celebrate Mother's Day and Father's Day. They're now being replaced by Special Person's Day, multi-faith Harmony Day and non-denominational, non-religious 'End of Year' celebrations.

I like the idea of Harmony Day – a multicultural country like Australia should teach kids to celebrate different cultures. But why should it replace Easter, which is a time of year much loved by children? The kids at my younger son's preschool weren't happy about the cancellation of the egg hunt at Easter under the new, more 'progressive' teaching regime. As you can imagine, they also didn't embrace the chocolate-free multi-faith celebration held in its place.

Same goes for Christmas. Yes, let's be inclusive and celebrate Hanukkah, Chinese New Year or Ramadan. But let's not lose Christmas. Half-arsed parents welcome inclusion and diversity but don't want to see the events and symbols that have been meaningful to many people over many years become black-banned in the name of 'progress'.

Educational settings, which are often at the forefront of social changes, have embraced this new offence-free, safety-first, politically correct world, removing anything that may challenge kids. Under one new national educational framework, children, rather than adults, are being given control over what they learn and how they learn. They are also no longer required to take part in end-of-year preschool concerts amid fears they get too stressed performing in front of others.

While this may be good for children with special needs, it sends the message to others that they can opt out of anything that may extend or challenge them. I understand kids need to be encouraged and supported by parents and teachers, but they also need to know who's boss. And they need to learn it's not them.

In the same vein, innocent preschool activities like 'show and tell' have been renamed as 'show and share' because kids aren't meant to tell others what they know but share their feelings and experiences. Staff have also stopped telling kids off and instead say things like 'make good choices, Ashton'. Activities have become free-choice. If a child doesn't want to do anything, like learn to hold a pencil, he or she doesn't have to. These days, the basics don't seem to matter. Instead, kids are given training to become 'champions of difference' and 'activists for equity' in their schools, childcare centres and preschools.

No wonder children these days are more anxious than ever; I suspect it's because they don't have enough boundaries and too many choices. Making matters worse are unfounded safety fears and concerns about litigation, further leading to the modification or banning of everyday children's events. In a suburb near me recently, a council threatened a man with a $1000 fine for having a basketball ring in his street. The fact that it had been up for two years, and was popular with adults and kids, didn't matter once a complaint had been received. Some councils are even banning basketball nets – but not the hoops – citing safety risks posed by kids with 'dental braces'. Everyone suffers because of the possibility of a non-existent unlikely risk that hasn't ever happened before. No one's stopping a kid with braces from pashing another kid with braces, which is much more of a safety risk.

It's a reflection of today's society, where no kid wins or loses, no one gets punished, and for every put-down they hear, they get three 'put-ups'.

Half-arsed parents aren't politically correct. They're sick of old customs being thrown aside in order to protect the precious feelings of people who probably don't care anyway. This approach turns normal things like lunchboxes and nursery rhymes into tests of our parenting and devotion. It reflects an obsession with small details and an overreaction to things that don't matter. This makes it harder for half-arsed parents to raise their kids the way they want because normal things have become suspect. And it makes it easier for hyper-vigilant, hyper-obsessive parents because it validates their choices and fears.

School bans

This scary new world is reflected in the vast array of items banned in many schools, including birthday cakes, hugs, spray-on deodorant, T-bar shoes, dogs, hoodies, beanies and sideburns. It reminds me of a headmistress at one Adelaide girls' school where I grew up who banned shoe polish as she thought shiny shoes would reflect the girls' undies and give the boys a thrill. These days, life-threatening allergies are causing schools to be nut-free, but some are taking it way too far, with items such as toilet rolls and egg cartons banned for hygiene and allergy reasons. In the playground, some schools have banned ball games and contact sports because they worry kids are going to get hurt.

In some cases, this is a matter of teachers going rogue and making up their own rules, but all too often the impetus for such silliness comes from parents trying to protect their kids from the nasties of modern life. You know, scary things like cakes, hugs and empty toilet paper rolls. Even homemade treats for a kids' birthday can be a no-go zone, with birthday hats and cardboard candles used instead. Oh great, I can't wait to celebrate my birthday at school by wearing a nit-ridden hat and blowing out pretend candles on a fake cake, SAID NO CHILD EVER.

Half-arsed parents think it's good that some things have changed. I am glad that teachers are no longer allowed to hit kids. But it should be okay for them to hug a child from time to time if they need comforting. We want kids to be active, but they can't play with balls or do sports involving contact with other kids at lunchtimes. We want kids to be healthy, but they can't bring fruit, eggs or dairy to some schools. You can send a child to school who hasn't been immunised, risking the spread of a deadly disease like typhoid fever. But schools are more obsessed about the risk posed by kids with food wrapped in cling wrap, kicking a footy at lunchtime and hugging their friends. It's completely ridiculous. Half-arsed parents don't have time for such petty obsessions.

Nursery rhymes

Preschools and childcare centres are little better, with some bringing in 'respectful nappy changing' guidelines, gender-neutral dress-up boxes with no boys' superhero and girls' princess costumes, and anatomically correct dolls. It's all so preachy and joyless. Nappy changes used to be about cleaning a bottom, not offering instruction in 'caring and closeness'.

One of the most grating symbols of this morose take on the world is the way books, songs and nursery rhymes are being tinkered with. I had dismissed claims nursery rhymes were being changed as a conservative conspiracy until I attended my younger son's music class a few years back. I was astonished to discover 'Baa Baa Black Sheep' had a modern makeover – he was no longer black, but red, green, blue and yellow. Black, it seems, is no longer an acceptable word, even to describe things that are black. And the children no longer sang the traditional words to the well-loved nursery rhyme. The words 'master' and 'dame' were removed as well – for what reason? Perhaps because they are gender-specific? Evidence of a hierarchical society? Who knows?

When questioned about the sheep's new technicolour 'do, my son's teacher assured me it wasn't a politically correct plot to indoctrinate kids into removing anything that could possibly be offensive, but a way to teach different colours. (Yeah, right.) She admitted the PC police have got their hands on a number of other well-known nursery songs. In the wonderful old song 'There was an old lady who swallowed a fly', the line 'perhaps she'll die' has been removed. Instead, the children sing, 'do you know why?'. The whole point of the song has been removed – along with the last line 'There was an old lady who swallowed a horse – she died, of course'.

Another much-loved song, which involved squashing imaginary fleas, has also been banned. The teacher was told by one parent, 'My child doesn't want to hurt anything' and so it was quietly dropped from the line-up of songs. Let's not blame the educators; teachers say many of the objections come from parents. Half-arsed parents think it's a pity. Children love these songs and games because they are silly and fun. Kids are smart enough to know it's not real life.

Children have a wonderful sense of the absurd that should be nurtured rather than ignored. They love it when we put a shoe on our head and pretend to wear it like a hat. They love using silly words like 'bum' and 'booger'. Changing songs like this may appear a minor concern, but it's indicative of a wider move to protect children from anything that may challenge them. Some places even add an extra verse which saves Humpty Dumpty from becoming an omelette. What's next? The Three Blind Mice getting cataract operations? The children who lived in the shoe having organic veggie wraps before hopping into bed early? Please, no. Half-arsed parents don't have time for all this. We like the originals and we're smart enough to cope with nursery rhymes where things get hurt, eaten and die. So are our kids. We don't want our precious childhood memories given a Disney make-over.

Changing books

Sadly, such attitudes are not confined to childcare centres, but are becoming commonplace in publishing too. Once upon a time, Dick was a boy, black was merely a colour and queer meant odd. This was back when there were no iPhones, no Xbox, no PS4 and

Candy Crush was what happened when you walked on lollies. Instead, kids played outside, made up adventures and read books. Lots of books. In our house, the number one choice were Enid Blyton books. (Well, apart from contraband copies of Judy Blume's *Forever* and Kathy Lette and Gabrielle Carey's *Puberty Blues*, but that's another story.)

When I was younger, I read about Noddy and Big Ears and didn't think it was odd they shared a bedroom. I didn't think they were gay. And I didn't think Big Ears was insulting to anyone who had protruding ears. I didn't think it was strange there was a boy called Dick, a girl called Fanny or a character called Dame Slap. Nor did I notice the alleged racial stereotyping involving a half-Spanish girl who was 'wild' and a French girl who was 'unscrupulous'.

All I found were wonderful, enjoyable stories filled with great adventures. Kids in the books weren't held back by modern irritants like over-protective 'drone' parenting, stranger danger and participation medals. Over the years, more people tinkered with the Blyton books I loved, removing words like tinker, which became 'traveller'. Dick became Rick, Fanny became Frannie and terms like 'wizard!', 'guffaw' and 'pooh-hah' were dropped altogether.

Words like queer and gay – which were used in their traditional sense – were taken out. And lines like 'That little ragamuffin gave me a good bang' or 'The pony went at a spanking trot' were removed. I accept some changes needed to be made. However, half-arsed parents don't want Enid Blyton or other authors cleaned up too much. We want to read these books and remember a time when kids played together, made their own fun and used their imagination. We want our kids to share these simpler times rather than the hyper-obsessive cottonwool era of today.

The words and characters of books like the *Famous Five* series reflect the era they were written in. Half-arsed parents are smart enough to see what's changed in society and what hasn't, and so are their children. How do kids learn about history if they can't see what times were like for children of other generations? The reader is immediately transported to an era that no longer exists, and that's part of the magic. Who's to say what came before wasn't better than now?

Book Week

Book Week or, as it's now known in many schools, Literacy Week, is another modern con that seems to exist to challenge parents rather than educate their kids. It's been around for years, but over time it's become less about reading and more an opportunity to judge parents on their crafting ability, creativity and willingness to devote six weeks to handmaking a costume.

Half-arsed parents who've struggled through the demands of Book Week know the pressure such events bring. They're supposed to be fun but often reduce confident parents to blithering messes. In most schools, children come dressed as their favourite book character, bring the relevant book and parade around in front of the rest of the school. Sounds simple, right? Don't be fooled. I've been doing this for ten years now, and I still can't get it right.

I was recently derailed by my younger son – who was all set to go as Batman – informing me at exactly 8.35 am there was a ban on superheroes. Yes, a ban. That's right, people, we have a common enemy, and it is a six-year-old with undies over his pants and a Batarang in his hand. That left us 15 minutes to think of a character from a book that took no effort, money or time. In the end, he tied a piece of shiny material over his shoulders left over from my daughter's *Little Miss Sunshine* dodgy dance phase and went as a magician. Then we spent the last ten minutes desperately trying to find a book about magic for him to take. (Harry Potter to the rescue once again.) Who needs pressure like this on a Wednesday morning?

Half-arsed parents see Book Week as the ultimate con of modern parenting, measuring our love and dedication one colour-matched sequin at a time. Is your child wearing a hand-sewn *Very Hungry Caterpillar* costume with the right number of legs? Top marks! You're a great parent who really cares about what makes your kids happy! Is your kid wearing normal clothes and carrying a copy of *Diary of a Wimpy Kid* grabbed at the last minute? You don't really love your kids, do you?

There are lots of parenting websites full of tips on how to sew, create and use hot-glue guns without getting third-degree burns. But no websites offer help for those who only remember Book Week on the day of the parade. Where's the advice for half-arsed parents who need to whip up a costume in five minutes with only items found in the vegetable crisper, the wardrobe and the linen closet? Where's the advice for parents of kids who don't want to dress-up, don't like reading and/or can't think of anyone to go as? And I've found no tips to help parents of kids who totally lose it ten minutes before they are due to leave as they discover the costume they thought they were going to wear no longer fits and they've lost the pirate sword/magician's wand/Harry Potter glasses.

I am really happy for the parents who have the time, money and skills to spend the best part of a month scouring op shops for accessories, doing 100 hours of sewing and spending 50 hours posting every step on Facebook. Good for them, and I mean that. It's a pity that some of them aren't as understanding of the need for half-arsed parents like me to hand our kid a saucepan as they walk out the door and make them go as Enid Blyton's Saucepan Man even though they have never heard of Enid Blyton.

The pressure of the day takes away from the books it's meant to be celebrating. Even better would be a Come to School Dressed in Pyjamas and Read Day. That's the kind of event half-arsed parents can get behind. Kids come to school dressed in pyjamas and bring along their favourite books. Older and younger kids are paired up and spend the day eating popcorn and lying around on beanbags reading. Let's hope it takes off. Then the mothers doing drop-off in their nighties can get out of the car for once.

Nude food

The trials of parenting today don't stop there. The parenting police are standing by, ready to judge mums and dads on the food they give their kids to take to preschool and school. These days, they don't just have to feed their kids healthy food, but items without wrappers – Nude Food. There are lots of different types of nudity. There's the good kind that happens between consenting adults on a Saturday morning when the kids are busy watching cartoons. There's the bad kind involving mature-age streakers at the races. And then there's the worst kind of all: Nude Food, and its celebratory event, Nude Food Day.

I was introduced to Nude Food Day when my son came home one day declaring that we must never, *ever* use any packaging in his lunchbox EVER again. The following day was Nude Food Day. 'We have to show our lunchboxes to the teachers and only people with no wrapping at all win a prize,' he told me, panicked as he eyed off the pile of plastic-wrapped sandwiches on the kitchen bench. By the way, Nude Food Day just happens to be sponsored by a company that makes the wrap-free lunchboxes.

Half-arsed parents think there's something really objectionable about making kids think the sky is going to fall in if they have sandwiches wrapped in cling wrap or foil. I'm not a big fan of teachers subjecting innocent kids to school-wide censure because they have a Vegemite and cheese sanga wrapped up to keep them fresh. I am a working mother, so often make lunches the night before, or a few days before and freeze them. This means I use lunch wrap. I feel like I'm at AA making a confession. My name is Susie O'Brien. I am a parent who uses sandwich wrap to keep my kids' food fresh.

Half-arsed parents don't want teachers auditing what we put in our children's lunchboxes. It's crazy. You audit someone for fiddling with their taxes or embezzling money, not for using cling wrap to keep a sandwich fresh or popping in an occasional sweet treat. And yet, preschool teachers in particular regularly monitor children's lunchboxes, sending home notes telling off parents for including a piece of chocolate cake or a homemade slice. One recent University of Melbourne study found photos of children with 'good' and 'bad' lunchboxes are circulated in some schools to teach others what to bring and what not to bring. Young students are also singled out by teachers and given yard duties or penalty points for having the wrong food, the study found. One girl buried a muesli bar in the playground because she was so embarrassed about having it in her lunchbox, and another had homemade cake returned with admonishment. Half-arsed parents are sick of such surveillance. They think it's their business – and no one else's – what their kids have in their lunchbox.

It wouldn't be such a problem if it were just a matter of popping a sandwich and an apple in a plastic container. Kids don't want daggy old supermarket lunchboxes. Now, nothing less than a container with a gel-top freezable section, an insulated 'cool skin' or 'chill out sock' will do. We don't have lunchboxes, we have 'insulated lunch solutions', 'thermal leak-proof containers' and 'stackable Bento boxes'. It's got to be BPA, PVC and waste-free *and* customised with the child's name on it. Whatever happened to basic plastic boxes with non-matching lids? Sure, parents can (and do) put their foot down and say no, but it's annoying that the bar has been raised so high.

Similarly, kids also don't want boring old sandwiches and fruit, with parents under pressure to make food exciting, creative and fun. This makes it our fault if the kids don't eat it because we haven't tried hard enough. I'm not buying it. I make this pledge to you as a half-arsed parent. My kids will never have food with faces drawn on it in a school lunchbox. They will not have sandwiches cut into funny shapes or made into mini nature scenes. There will be no themes, no excitement, no creativity. And definitely no zucchini zoodles. Their lunchboxes will continue to contain good plain food they are expected to eat. Or go hungry. I will not tie a ribbon around green beans to make them fun and zany. I will not 'seduce', 'entertain' and 'excite' my kids through their lunchboxes. I will just feed them. That's the half-arsed way. Step away from the zucchini and put down the spiraliser. Feels better, doesn't it?

Such initiatives change the goalposts, turning normal things into tests of our commitment and ability as parents. Half-arsed parents pay no attention to such matters. They use cling wrap without fear or favour, and tell their kids to make their own costumes for Book Week. They think it's okay that Baa Baa is a black sheep and they giggle over characters called Dick.

Chapter 6

MUMMY WARS

Half-arsed parents ignore judgmental advice from others about how to raise their kids. Some mothers seem keen to establish themselves as the fount of all child-raising knowledge. It's not just about detailing what they do, but convincing others that theirs is the best way, the only way to bring up children. Invariably, they go about the task with the zeal of Mormon missionaries, only with more expensive outfits and fewer polyester pantsuits. Celebrity mums are leading the way. They aren't happy with eating their own placentas, letting five-year-olds suck on their boobs or going through a 36-hour labour drug-free; they want to recruit others to their cause.

Welcome to the mummy wars. It's a world where mothers are divided and win by conquering others. UK researcher Dr Kate Orton-Johnson calls it the 'new momism' which pits mother against mother in a 'lose–lose situation for women'. She's right. Not only do the mummy wars ignore the diversity of mothers, but they place women in oppositional categories to be compared, judged and found wanting. It's the antithesis of half-arsed parenting. Half-arsed mums and dads are too busy trying to remember what day of the week it is, whose house their kids stayed at the night before and whether it's a pupil-free day at school to care what other parents are doing.

The New Republic magazine forecast the advent of the Daddy Wars back in 2013, but they haven't happened yet. Fathers are more averse to casting judgy-judgy glances at other dads for their choice of pram or the fact that their sprog is sucking from a sweet apple and blackcurrant pouch rather than homemade goo the colour of diarrhoea. Perhaps this is because the standards are lower for dads. As US comedian Ali Wong says, 'It takes so little to be considered a great dad, and it also takes so little to be considered a shitty mom.'

In the mummy wars, most types of mothering are based on a model that puts raising kids above everything else: work, relaxation, partners and friends. Dads have never been expected to live up to this high bar. But any mother who doesn't make the kid the centre of their existence is often made to feel inadequate.

Not buying into the mummy wars is a key part of the half-arsed parenting approach; don't try to be too perfect, don't follow ridiculous rules set down by people you haven't even met, and don't feel like you're letting your kids down because you're not following the latest organic/superfood/attachment parenting fad. Much better sources of advice are your best friend, mum, dad, GP and maternal health nurse. And maybe your horoscope, if that's your thing. If you are guided as a Pisces by the moon's ascendance in your celestial quadrant, go for it.

Here are some of the mummies you'll see battling it out for uber-mum status.

Yummy mummies

Some see the high-water mark as the yummy mummy, who's sexually attractive and well groomed. One study found new mothers felt great pressure to 'bounce back' and lose weight straight after giving birth. In other words, to not look like a mother. 'Women felt strengthened through motherhood but looking like a mother was not considered worth pursuing,' researcher Dr Christina Prinds concluded. The implication is that mothers can look like mothers, but only yummy ones, not the ones in yesterday's fleece with food stains on the collar.

Yummy mummies are there to make everyone else look bad by appearing perfect in every way. Even in jeans and a casual shirt, they look a million dollars. Or a thousand at least, because that's what their True Religion jeans and Sass and Bide top cost. Their boys are called Sebastian and Rufus, and their girls Sigrid and Octavia, and they're in denial about the fact that they're the biggest bullies in the school. These mums spend their days on Facebook posting about all the gifted and amazing things their little brutes do, like blink and breathe at the same time.

This style of mothering was elevated in the Australian TV series *Yummy Mummies* which demonstrated that having a baby is no barrier to being stylish and beautiful and lording it over other parents. These mums have genetically blessed offspring, suspiciously pert breasts and $1500 baby bags. The show's trailer depicted a baby shower complete with bouquets of $100 notes, chandeliers, horse-drawn carriages and baby-scan helium balloons. 'Does everyone need to see inside your uterus?' one of the mums asks the baby shower host. Yes, it seems, they do. Not surprisingly, the show was widely slammed for its unrealistic and offensive expectations and for presenting babies as another designer accessory. You know, like a Hermes Birkin, but smellier.

While Burberry baby clothes are out of reach for most mums, there's a yummy mummy at every price point and suburban location. Motherhood sure has changed. No one expected 70s mums with their Dr Scholl's sandals, hairy legs and bra-free boobs to look hot. Now, to be a successful mother, you have to be sexy and high maintenance. Mothers' groups provide another KPI, with friendships won and lost according to the ability of the yummy mummy to squeeze back into her pre-baby jeans by the six-week mark. And she'd better not have any unfashionable accessories (like work-from-home husbands and vinyl Jason recliners) lying around when it's her turn to host the other mums.

Half-arsed mothers can't be bothered with such crap, but they'll make friends with the yummy mummies from the school so they can borrow something decent to wear to the races.

Natural mothers

Natural mothers breastfeed until the child decides he or she has had enough, let the kids sleep in bed with them and wear their babies in a sling around the clock. This style of mothering was immortalised in a 2012 US *Time* cover story which asked: 'Are you mom enough?' It attracted attention, mainly because it had an attractive blonde on the cover breastfeeding her three-year-old, who was standing on a chair so he could reach his mother's boobs. Author Kate Pickert profiled mums whose lives were all about their kids. One left her child for the first time only when she went into hospital to have her second. Most of the time half-arsed parents can't wait to escape their kids, so you won't find us wearing them 24 hours a day. Half-arsed parents see hospital stays as a blessed release and believe in things like childcare, cots, prams and childfree nights out that end at 3 am. Oh, and breastfeeding that stops well before the kid is old enough to do it standing up.

Natural mothers are also known as attachment mothers, or even Zen mothers. 'God grant me the serenity to accept the things I cannot change,' the Zen mother's mantra goes. Half-arsed parents also accept the things they cannot change, like their daughter's nappy because they're on a plane and they've run out of Huggies. There's an article on natural parenting on a website called 'Raised Good: Parenting by Nature'. Ignore, for a moment, that it should be called 'Raised Bad: Parenting by People With Poor Grammar'. It says that natural parents are raising their kids 'the way Mother Nature wanted'. Well, I'll bet Mother Nature didn't have to cope with some of the evils of modern life, like corn syrup, phone apps that are more addictive than meth and mothers who hang around during play dates instead of dumping their kids and running.

Half-arsed parents do not want their kids to 'reach milestones in their own time' like natural parents do. Ideally, we want our kids to be potty-trained, use the toaster and master an iPad by the time they're five months old so we can stay in bed longer in the mornings. The website tells me natural parents 'seek to strengthen their attachment with their children, no matter the circumstance'. Half-arsed mums in particular want more time away from the little buggers, not less. 'Infants are more likely to form secure attachments when their distress is responded to promptly, consistently and appropriately,' the website tells me. Yeah, they're also likely to be still living at home at 28.

Half-arsed parents don't want to 'practice natural, positive parenting'. They believe in discipline, along with food bribes and letting kids wear the same shabby superhero and princess dress-ups for three years, if they want to. One book about positive parenting is by a woman called Sara Deedley who wants us to 'become the parents that children love to spend time with'. What kind of self-obsessed crap is this? Half-arsed parents are the ones children love to escape from because they're boring and unfun, especially before the first coffee or three.

Attachment Parenting International says parents who treat their babies with love, compassion and respect are 'literally wiring their children's brains for empathy, trust and the ability to self-regulate stress'. Yes, and they're also the kind of parents who can't talk about anything but their kids, only get three broken hours of sleep a night and have four days' worth of high-tide breastmilk stains on their tops. Some natural parents believe in elimination communication, which sees them try and 'respond to their babies' bodily needs' by rushing them off to the toilet every five seconds rather than letting them use nappies. This turns them into stressed-out zombies hiding out in darkened rooms, waiting for their baby to give them another 'signal' that they're ready to do a bowel movement. Half-arsed parents do not see a poonami of epic proportions as anything other than a shit. Same goes for mealtimes. Half-arsed parents don't want to 'feed with love and respect'. They want to feed with food, when a child is hungry. It's a meal, not a religious experience.

There's an offshoot of natural parenting called RIE Parenting, which stands for Resources for Infant Educators. The RIE (pronounced 'rye') mob go even further. Be afraid, people. Very afraid. RIE parents 'involve their babies in their own caregiving from the very beginning in order to take some of the pressure off'. 'Begin by talking to your baby and treating them like a dignified person rather than a helpless infant from day one,' RIE experts advise. When it comes to nappy changing, 'RIE parents not only tell their baby what they are about to do, but they also ask for permission'. If the baby doesn't give consent, what then? Does the dirty nappy stay on? Half-arsed parents will never ask permission from any of their babies before changing their nappies, you can be sure of that. When I was on the RIE website, ads for flat non-leather shoes – you know, the kind that act as natural contraceptives – came up. This tells you all you need to know about this form of parenting. Even Google wants RIE parents to be too unattractive to procreate.

Celebrity mothers

It's harder to escape celebrity mothers, who take the mummy wars to a whole new level. Many celebs feel inspired, in fact *compelled*, to share their mothering journeys because they feel as if they are the only ones who have ever had a baby. They have so much wisdom and beauty that it would be a shame for them not to inspire those who are unlucky enough not to be them. They see motherhood as the culmination of their life's achievements and a spiritual calling. This doesn't stop them from selling their baby photos to *Who Weekly* for $150,000. They think you need them to share their positive messages of peace, wisdom and paid product placements. They also don't let their lack of knowledge about biology, health, medicine or nutrition stop them from spruiking their eponymous skincare range at every possible opportunity.

In *The Mommy Myth*, Susan J. Douglas and Meredith W. Michaels argue that celebrity role models undermine women because of the great chasm between the image they promote and the reality of everyday life. I couldn't agree more. Celebrity mothers on million-dollar salaries who hawk their maternal perfection prey on other women's insecurities. They go on about how much they eat normally when in fact they haven't ingested solid food for three years, and their guiltiest pleasure is driving past McDonald's and taking a whiff of boiling fat. They claim breastfeeding made them lose weight when they've been working out with their trainer five hours a day. They make appearing on the red carpet look effortless when in fact it's preceded by a two-day wheatgrass fast and colonic irrigation. They talk about how much they love their family when in reality their kids no longer talk to them and their partner spends most of their time locked inside the pool house getting one-on-one tantric yoga coaching with someone called Ki.

Half-arsed mothers know they have to tune out the celebrity crap. They have enough guilt in their lives without the added burden of finding 3 am feeds 'precious' like Angelina Jolie. Few have the luxury of taking extended unpaid leave or never going back to work like actor Kate Hudson, who 'swore long ago she wasn't going to leave any doubt in her children's minds that they came first and work came second'. Apparently, it's okay to have a paid job as well as be a mum – as long as you let everyone know you truly want to be at home with your kids.

The initial phase of isolation and lockdown brought out the worst in celebrities, who seemed shocked to be in the same boat as everyone else. Of course, their boat was a $10 million yacht while ours was a one-oared rubber dinghy with a slow leak. 'We're all in this together,' they told us from their sprawling rural properties, chic inner-city bolt-holes and gated mega mansions. They acted as if we ordinary folk needed them to help us feel grateful. They thought that without their wise counsel, inspiring homilies and beauty product suggestions, we wouldn't have the strength to get through Covid. But I can assure you that parents with bed hair trying to look professional on Zoom work calls did not feel inspired by *Wonder Woman* actor Gal Gadot sending a message of hope from her walk-in closet. 'Staying home is my super power,' she said. Well, I'm a working mother-of-three and my super power is ignoring my offspring who spent their days in isolation fighting about who ate the leftovers from the fridge and whose turn it was to feed the dog.

And remember stars such as Sia, Jimmy Fallon, Will Ferrell, Kristen Wiig and Natalie Portman each singing

Celebrity vs half-arsed

Celebrity says: *I like to rise with the sun – there's a certain sanity which comes with getting up at first light.*

Half-arsed mum says: I don't like to rise when the alarm goes off at 6 am but I have no choice. There's a certain sanity that comes from wearing earplugs so I can't hear the kids arguing.

Celebrity says: *I walk as much as I can.*

Half-arsed mum says: I walk as little as I can. I have been known to drive three blocks from my house to drop the kids at school.

Celebrity says: *For brekkie I have wholegrain toast or an eggwhite omelette.*

Half-arsed mum says: For brekkie I have Vegemite toast if the kids have left me any bread. I once ordered an eggwhite omelette but it tasted like snot.

Celebrity says: *On party-free days, I make sure I am properly nourished, have a run and sleep properly.*

Half-arsed mum says: On party-free days, I make sure I am properly nourished thanks to leftover UberEats, and I sleep as late as the kids will let me. The only thing running in my house is the fridge.

Celebrity says: *I am very lucky to have a gym super close by!*

Half-arsed mum says: The closest fitness centre we have is full of fat old people doing arm raises in a lukewarm wee-filled toddler pool!

Celebrity says: *I do a lot of body weight resistance. I also love kettlebell work.*

Half-arsed mum says: I do a lot of resisting weight-loss. I also love kettle chips.

Celebrity says: *Even time-poor mums can lose weight and tone up with a little bit of planning and preparation.*

Half-arsed mum says: Even time-poor mums can lose weight if they cut off a limb or two and tone up by wearing fat-squashing Spanx!

Celebrity says: *Another great way to get back into shape is to use your baby as your weights.*

Half-arsed mum says: I once tried to exercise using a baby as a dumbbell but the mother complained and I had to give him back.

Celebrity says: *You can also do squats while holding your baby or lay him on the floor and do push-ups over the top of him.*

Half-arsed mum says: You can also have sleeps while holding your baby, or lay on the floor and do absolutely nothing while your baby lies on top of you.

a line from the John Lennon song *Imagine*? It was designed to unite us, and unite us it did – in agreement that none of them can sing, and shouldn't try. It also united us in the feeling that a bunch of multimillionaires shouldn't be singing about imagining life with 'no possessions' when dole queues were longer than they had been since the Great Depression. We also didn't need singer Lizzo to help us with our 'healing from fear during this global crisis'. In fact, what we needed was healing from tone-deaf celebrities. I was too busy wiping coffee off the walls thanks to my teenage daughter's experiments with whipped espressos to be inspired by the fact that Lizzo could twerk and play a flute at the same time.

Many celebrity mothers want to share their brand of bohemian sugar-free 'conscious' parenthood. Leading the boho mama pack is actor Teresa Palmer. In a recent *Vogue* magazine article, she's wearing a floaty designer dress and cavorting barefoot on a riverbank with a gentle breeze stirring her softly tousled hair. She's with her colour-matched, tow-haired offspring who have perfected the art of looking cute on cue. They're boys so of course they're bare-chested and wearing jewellery. No Target bargain-bin cast-offs for them. Where's the lurid plastic wading pool full of balls, lost Matchbox cars and stale wee? The kid who's screaming and refusing to smile because you've taken the iPad away and Peppa Pig hadn't finished yet? The *Vogue* story tells me motherhood and movies are what defines Palmer. These are 'what has transformed her into the woman she is today: a veritable Earth Mother who juggles many roles – mother, wife, actor, activist, friend.' (Note the pecking order of roles here.)

As a half-arsed parent, I am proud to admit that white wine and Smith's chicken chips are what define me and what have transformed me into the woman I am today. I am a working mother who juggles many roles – servant, taxi driver, ATM and reality TV fan who'd prefer to watch cooking shows than make dinner. Palmer, *Vogue* says, is a 'poster woman for modern mothers' thanks to her ability to be a 'blonde, blue-eyed actress working her way up the Tinseltown ladder'. Well, I'm happy to be a poster woman for half-arsed real parents. My blonde hair has a delightful touch of both mouse brown and grey at the roots, my blue eyes are bloodshot from lack of sleep and the only ladder I'm climbing is the one that helps me get soccer balls off the roof.

The half-arsed new mum will also run a mile from parenting advice from actor Alicia Silverstone. Silverstone's book *The Kind Mama* is a vegan attachment-parenting manifesto that dismisses nappies as 'pseudoscience' and urges women to enjoy placenta smoothies. In Silverstone's eyes, tampons are making us infertile, cots are 'barred-in boxes' that lead to child neglect and children should be left to do their business 'on the grass'. Silverstone tells us that eating 'kind foods' – i.e. plants – can cure post-natal depression. 'Some women experience the blues after giving birth,' she writes, but it is 'less common among kind mamas.'

Half-arsed parents ignore such bat-shit crazy advice, even from a former Batgirl. They know post-partum depression is a serious medical condition, and not just the 'baby blues'. Silverstone reduces it to something that can be merely eaten away. But what can you expect from a woman who uses words like 'baby house' to describe her uterus and calls her vagina a 'hoo-ha' or a 'chichi'? It sounds like she's gone a bit crazy after spending too much time lying awake in a pool of her son's wee thanks to her belief in both natural toileting and co-sleeping. Half-arsed parents don't fall for such rubbish. They're proudly committed to nappies, cots and seeking proper medical advice for serious illnesses.

Mummy tribes

You may not come across yummy mummies, natural mums or celebs in your everyday life, but they aren't the only ones judging half-arsed parents with their sad little disapproving faces and sanctimonious horseshit. Some other mummy tribes are a lot closer to home – in fact, they're waiting for you at the school gate right now. Here's a guide to some of the wacky, wonderful and downright weird parents out there.

Fashionistas

Elle Macpherson doing school drop-off in stylish designer outfits a few years ago set a new standard for playground attire. It may be 8 am, but fabulous femmes like her sport false eyelashes, velvet pantsuits with plunging necklines and chandeliers for earrings. Their kids have exotic European names like Consuela and Brunetti and they're never seen in a Ben Ten T-shirt or anything from Kmart's pole-dancing range. They died of shame when their daughters wanted Elsa's *Frozen 2* dresses for Christmas.

Known for: Trying to pash the principal at the parents' drinks night after sculling a bottle of Veuve Clicquot in the car park.

Celebrity hero: Elle, of course

Working mums

They'd love to have a latte with you after drop-off but they've got a Middle East peace deal to broker by lunchtime. They're always nicely dressed in their city suits and sensible heels but are too busy to get to know anyone. They're always over-stretched, and frazzled as they realise they've forgotten to pack lunches for the kids and missed the 7.35 am city train. Again. But wait until they discover your kids are friends and you live in the same street. Then they'll bombard you with last-minute requests for emergency play dates, help with drop-off and reminders about where the school actually is.

Known for: Being really nice when they finally have the time to get to know you, and giving ridiculously generous donations to the annual school gala out of guilt.

Celebrity hero: Amal Clooney

Gym junkies

These women are smarter than they look, trust me. Their moisture-wicking three-way-stretch three-quarter organic yoga pants cost $350 but make them look ten kilos lighter without doing any exercise. These lithe lasses fill their days picking up large tubs of protein shakes from the health shop, getting spray tans and drinking skinny soy chai lattes. If you want to hang with them, be willing to spend hours debating the relative merits of the Blaze versus the Surge Fitbit. And if they ask you how long you can hold a plank, be warned it's nothing to do with picking up a piece of wood.

Known for: Not going to the gym very often, but that doesn't matter because they look the part.

Celebrity hero: Jessica Alba

Fitness fanatics

Unlike gym junkies, fitness fanatics are too busy to be at the school gate because they've got an endless round of Pilates, interval training, high-intensity and vibration fitness (which I'll bet isn't as much fun as it sounds) classes to get to. Luckily, they're also too busy to judge you for your bed hair and saggy-bottomed trackie pants. The problem is that they're also unlikely to notice anyone crossing the road when they're trying to get their BMW 4WD into a tight parking spot in front of their gym.

Known for: Banging on about PBs.

Celebrity hero: Michelle Bridges

Kathmandu crew

Yes, that is a nightie peeking out of their fleecy top. Yes, these are slippers, but don't tell anyone. These mums are too busy making mountain bread wraps with organic spelt flour and heirloom vegetables to get dressed for drop-off. They're also too busy picketing city streets about global warming to get the kids to school on time or change their clothes. This is why you want them as pals. They make you look good.

Known for: The banana kale bran muffins that they bring to class parties that taste like wallpaper paste and turn everyone's poo green for a week.

Celebrity hero: Al Gore

Competitive bakers

The 80s supermum syndrome has abated, but it's been replaced with the super homemaker. Holding down paid employment is too much pressure and eats too much into crafting time for these ladies. Instead, they stay home and create web-based businesses selling printed nursery artworks ripped off Etsy. As their kids age, they fill their days producing exquisite themed birthday parties that they secretly think are spoiled by the presence of children. Of course, they know nothing they do is worth anything unless it's admired by less-talented mums on social media, so they spend a lot of time on Instagram.

They're known for: Posts showing their delicate handmade cupcakes with the caption: 'How did I ever find the time to work!!!!'

Celebrity hero: Martha Stewart

Organic obsessives

Back in the 70s, it was all about consciousness-raising: helping women see how they are enslaved by the patriarchal society. These women are now railing against a new enemy – additives, processed food and anything with a food mile in double figures. They're so obsessive that their idea of a good time isn't nudity and nooky, but nude food and lunchbox checks at kindergarten. They're happy to pay six times more for their organic misshapen apples, as long as they get to boast to other parents about how 'healthful' their kids are.

They're known for: Offering to give presentations to the school community about the importance of FODMAP.

Celebrity hero: Pete Evans

School dads

Dads can be school mums too – just ask them. There aren't many fathers at most drop-offs so they really stand out. The ones wearing tight athletic compression pants without shorts over the top *definitely* stand out. Some school dads are between jobs and spend their time frowning into their phones and wishing they were somewhere else. Other dads are happy to be at pick-up. They'll bang on about how their mates think they hang out in the park all day on social media. Then they take the kids to the park where they'll pass the time composing witty tweets about fatherhood.

Known for: Having a bit of a chip on his shoulder and, on a bad day, lots of chips on his shoulders thanks to the toddler food bribes that helped get him to pick-up on time.

Celebrity hero: Ryan Reynolds' Twitter feed

Half-arsed parents can't be bothered with such competitive rubbish. Some days we're a bit gym junkie, a bit supermodel and a bit yummy mummy. Half-arsed parents know they can't make assumptions about people based on their clothes, hair and the quality of their baked goods. That crazy-haired harpy in the corner of the school grounds going on about the quality of the canteen food probably won a Nobel prize for her searing analysis of the global trade wars and is Amal Clooney's best friend.

Half-arsed parents try not to get sucked into the madness. They don't think mums and dads have to agree about everything and get along at all times. They are respectful to other parents, as long they're not trying to guilt them, preach to them or convert them. They figure everyone's probably doing their best, and that's all you can ask for, isn't it? If half-arsed parents don't have anything nice to say, they keep quiet, or they go rogue and write a book . . .

Chapter 7

SOCIAL MEDIA MADNESS

Another key part of half-arsed parenting is ignoring the perfect lives presented by other parents on social media. If you think school parents are hard, you should meet this mob. As Kathy Walker, author of *Future-proofing Your Child*, says, social media 'offers very quick access to all the amazing things other parents are doing in order to impress others'. She's right. In the past, you had to pick up the phone or see someone in person to brag about how great your life was. And then you had to find subtle ways to weave your superiority into conversation. For example: 'Oh, Chloe and Charlie are so naughty. They have competitions to see who's a faster slalom skier when we spend our annual month at the snow. And they are complaining our mountain-top chalet is too small! Oh, kids!' Now you just head to Fakebook – oops, I mean Facebook – and say the same thing to 2500 people at once.

Social media mums post pithy sayings such as, 'Your greatest contribution to the universe may not be something you do, but someone you raise'. Well, my greatest contribution to the universe is raising kids who aren't dickheads. This is because they don't have a mother who's socially insecure and makes them pose with kale and avocado cupcakes that match their $500 green T-shirts. As a mother, I don't care about 'retaining my sensuality' and 'finding my femininity' like some social media influencers. I care about retaining my sanity and finding my daughter's mouthguard that cost $80.

Mothers spend a lot more time following other mums on social media than dads, which makes them much more susceptible to the negative messages and social pressure. Women aged 18 to 29 are more likely to use social media sites such as Snapchat and Instagram than any other demographic, while older women tend to use Facebook. Women spend more time than men updating, managing and maintaining their social media profiles. If they are anything like me, they also spend more time trying not to get offended about the ads that keep popping up in their social media feeds for dating sites, control-top underwear and orthopaedic surgeons. Just for the record, I am not single, living in St Kilda and in need of a knee operation.

Frequent exposure to social media results in high levels of weight dissatisfaction, a drive for thinness and increased body surveillance in women. This is especially the case with sites showcasing photos of muscled mums with six-pack abs and toned thighs. Flinders University researchers found these so-called 'fitspiration' images lead to increased negative mood in mothers. As my daughter would say, 'No shit, Sherlock.' Who wants to have these women telling us how to look?

Many are mothers who pose with their young children in order to show parenthood is no barrier to being super-fit and muscular. Fitspo slogans include 'some mums lift more than just their kids' and 'a baby is a reason, not an excuse'. Some even use their kids as weights or barbells. Remember Maria Kang, the buffed American mum who posed with her three young boys with the caption 'What's your excuse?'? She was widely panned for guilting other mothers who don't have the time or inclination to bench-press their offspring for 45 minutes before breakfast.

Selfies have the same impact. Posting selfies on social media makes women feel anxious, unconfident and unattractive, even when the photos have been retaken and retouched. 'It is likely that scrutinising and modifying images of themselves makes women think more about their flaws and imperfections,' researcher Professor Marika Tiggemann says. 'It is also likely that selfie-posting makes women think about how they look from others' perspective and how they will be judged, encouraging self-objectification.' Selfie takers also think a lot about how their photos look, but they don't think much about how silly they look standing with a selfie stick on the edge of a ravine.

Insta influencers

Instagrammers let the pictures do the talking. Mostly this is because they've got nothing much to say. It's a realm where delusion and unjustified entitlement reign supreme. These Insta influencers don't work; they select a handful of contorted poses, hold a product and gaze dreamily into the middle distance. For this they may be paid many thousands of dollars. Their job description seems to be wearing bikinis, posing on the edge of pools and writing captions while intoxicated. In an ideal world, they quit their jobs and travel the world full-time, staying in luxury resorts in return for picture-perfect posts delivered directly to their 100,000 plus followers. It's not a freebie, darling; it's a *collaboration*. Or, as the influencers call it, a co-lab.

Covid has been hard on these talentless nobodies. Thanks to travel restrictions and lockdown, they've been reduced to soulful bathroom selfies and inspirational affirmations. Looking picture-perfect in tight lycra, they will urge you to 'believe in yourself'. They want us to know they're 'agile' and they've 'pivoted' – by this they mean they've been doing yoga three times a day on sponsored brand-name mats. But it's not easy. How are they expected to meet their public's insatiable appetite for their hair-treatment tips and brand-name lifestyle products from their living rooms? And there's always the big issue of the day to deal with: does a beetroot quinoa matcha latte even exist if no one is there to watch you drink it? Half-arsed parents need to forget about perfect Insta-mums with their try-hard lives and rock-hard abs. If they really were as happy and secure as they make out, they'd remember to wear clothes when they have their photo taken.

The best influencers make sure their followers know they're not perfect by showing how crappy they look without make-up at 3 am. Then they make sure they look extra gorgeous in the next ten posts. Take Sophie Cachia, who's got more than 250,000 followers on Instagram. She posts as 'The Young Mummy' and offers a refreshing but picture-perfect view of motherhood. Cachia says sex is her favourite form of exercise and the best present she's ever received is contraception. And yet her posts are heavily styled and not achievable for the average mum, let alone a young mum. Even a recent marriage breakdown and sexuality crisis didn't dim the abundance of gorgeousness Cachia presents. In one apparently casual photo, her Louis Vuitton bag is perched prominently on the desk and she sports perfect make-up and glossy curls. I bought Louis Vuitton once, but everyone knew it was fake because there was only one t in 'Vuitton'.

But there's no denying the reach of these influencers. A Flinders University study of 220 female Australian university students found looking at Instagram images with a high number of likes makes them feel good about their own looks. But being highly invested in getting likes on their own photos makes them feel bad. Young girls and women aged 14 to 24 feel the greatest pressure to get likes on their posts, and the American Psychological Association has even linked social media competition to a rise in youth suicide rates.

Yet these pesky, pert self-promoters are more popular than ever, especially if they have what's considered to be 'authentic' content. But there's nothing very genuine about many Insta influencers and their sparkly rainbow lives. A recent *Vanity Fair* article about social media mums from Byron Bay – dubbed the 'murfers', the mother surfers – was a huge talking point because it illustrated the vast chasm between image and reality. *Vanity Fair* dubbed these women 'mid-tier family lifestyle micro-influencers' and savaged them for their hypocrisy.

The murfers go on about raising their tech-free kids naturally and yet they have a very highly curated social media presence. They bang on about being natural and authentic, but they're using their kids in paid posts as advertising fodder. They go on about living a blessed existence full of surfing sessions and organic linen outfits, but it's only possible because of trust funds and family money. No doubt the article caused some personal angst, but it also drove other women to the murfers' Insta sites for bigger doses of their all-natural millionaire beachy lifestyles. It's a sign of the importance of social media in the lives of many mothers.

Here's how these and other Insta influencers suck us in.

They have amazing lives

Insta-mums lead whimsical, magical lives thanks to the #endlesslove from their offspring called Thelma, Narkita and Caspar. They share travel tips, assure us mere mortals that first class is 'worth it alone for the cashmere PJs' and spend a ridiculous amount of time barely dressed in picturesque tropical locations. The sun is always shining and their kids don't refuse to pose in spotless outfits for take after take. They spend their Saturday afternoons making heart shapes with their hands against the sunset and posing next to picturesque painted walls in inner-city laneways. Good luck trying to get my kids doing this. Captions are often motivational mantras such as 'Do something today your future self will thank you for'. No one will know what they mean, but it sounds deep.

They are #blessed

These Insta influencers live in a world foreign to most of us: a land of white couches, matching clothing and ice cream that always goes with the child's outfits. The only time half-arsed kids' clothes match their food is when they spill what they're eating down their tops. Most challenging to me are the spiritual Insta-mums, who are #beyondblessed to have perfect, devoted husbands and beautiful, healthy kids. They make sure people know how amazing their life is by providing captions such as, 'When you are flown in your private helicopter onto a rock of fire to do yoga'. But they always let people know they are really down-to-earth with #blessed #spiritanimal hashtags. If they are having a bad day and can't get out of bed, they declare it to be 'Throwback Thursday' and post pictures from last year when they looked hotter than they do now.

They're masters of the #isobrag

Covid and isolation brought out the worst in everyday Insta-mums as well. While most families in lockdown were reduced to eating mac 'n' cheese in stained dressing gowns and screaming about who's using all the wi-fi, Insta-mums were keen to show us how they were nailing it. In immaculate, light-filled houses they wanted us to know they were rediscovering the joy of family togetherness, one 1000-piece jigsaw puzzle at a time. 'Just doing what we can', they captioned photos of their kids delivering scones in rattan baskets, looking like a cross between Florence Nightingale and Martha Stewart before she went to jail. Everyone knew about their selfless sacrifice but no one knew the scones were hard as rocks and full of last night's leftovers scraped off plates. These isobraggers posted about the doughnuts they'd baked from scratch during a break from home schooling, videos of their kitchen table art classes and their $110 takeaway box from a three-star restaurant that came with 13 pouches, instructions on plating up and a curated Spotify playlist. They didn't care that in isolation I often paid $130 for UberEats Chinese delivered 45 minutes late by a man in a Hyundai Getz.

Half-arsed parents aren't fooled. They know most of what appears on social media is a very selective version of reality. Rather than try to emulate B-listers with F-cups in G-strings, they get on with enjoying life and being honest about what they do and don't do. It's all about getting back to basics and tuning out all the bullshit. Embrace wrinkles, work up a sweat, dance up a storm, eat great food without taking photos of it first, listen to music, have fun with your kids, work hard and spend time with good friends and family. Live, laugh, love and make mistakes. Half-arsed parents know that's what's real, not looking orgasmic while posing for photos with your bum in the air.

Say no to Fakebook

Instagram influencers are not the only ones making things hard for everyone else. Half-arsed parents also have to contend with everyday mums and dads sharing every mundane and made-up aspect of their lives on Facebook, which I call Fakebook. A lot of studies show that Fakebook sucks us into its competitive vortex. Those who are already a teensy bit neurotic are most at risk of feeling depressed when they check out the perfect lives everyone else seems to be living.

We've all got friends who post group photos on Fakebook showing them looking young and beautiful while everyone else has double chins and bra straps hanging out. Who needs pals like that? I swear, if anyone else puts pictures of themselves lying on tropical beaches with captions like, 'Another mojito, please', I'll stab myself in the eye with a cocktail umbrella. It's even worse when you are the one still at work. I don't want to know that my friends are on a kick-arse tropical island knocking back cosmos while I am on level 12 knocking back advances from the photocopier repairman. They should also spare us the details of their annoying travel disappointments. Trust me, no one is sympathetic about international flight delays leading to more time in the first-class lounge ('Free food!!') or the fact that they had to line up for 20 minutes to get their accommodation upgrade for their luxury London hotel. This was even more annoying during lockdown when Melburnians were limited to only leaving their house for one hour a day within a 5 km radius during the worst of winter. Trust me, we weren't even vaguely interested in how unseasonably hot the weather was in Cairns.

I don't begrudge my friends the right to go on holiday, but I wish they would do it somewhere boring and cold. I can't tell you the excitement I felt seeing the following post in my Fakebook feed. 'Big, long, pointless drive. Feeling lousy but had to get out. Giant fibreglass marsupial.' People should post as much as they like if their holiday involves spending lots of time in a car travelling to destinations such as Australia's longest single-track lattice girder bridge or a museum featuring artwork made in the 19th century of human hair. Sucks to be you, my friends.

An expert Fakebooker will hide their boasting in an apparently well-meaning post. Don't be fooled: an innocent missive about a sunrise a couple of your friends saw while jogging is actually an exercise in demonstrating their moral and social status. Let's unpack it. First, they went jogging. Second, they are staying at a beach with some spectacular views. Third, they are the kind of people who get up before dawn to stay fit. Fourth, you weren't invited and they don't care that you know it. That's Fakebook for you.

Half-arsed parents know they won't ever see a post showing the same friend tearing into a packet of Twisties while downing half a cask of chardy on the couch the night before, crying because her husband hasn't come home. On Fakebook, you rarely ever get the full picture because it undermines the life people want you to think they live. You don't hear about the horrific mess left behind in the kitchen after your friend made a batch of reindeer cupcakes with little pretzels for antlers. Or the family fight at the winery after Auntie Dot discovered Uncle Allan put a nip of gin in the baby's sippy cup to make her sleep. Or the 40-minute back-to-school photoshoot from the mother trying to make her kids look genuinely and spontaneously happy for the benefit of women she went to school with 20 years ago. Half-arsed parents should remember: you didn't like them then, and you shouldn't worry about them now.

I look at some of my friends' social media posts and wonder who the hell they really are. Who hasn't answered 'I'm fine' when really you want to say something like, 'My kids are giving me the shits and my husband is never home. This morning we had no margarine or toilet paper and I realised I forgot to tape *Love Island* and will be home from work too late to watch it live. My best friend rang to tell me she has to get a biopsy on a weird lump under her arm and my favourite work pants don't fit me any more.' That night, you'll put up a carefree post on Fakebook debating whether you should go to Paris or Phuket on your next family holiday.

Half-arsed parents are more honest. They share their ups and downs on social media, not just the highlights. Their posts do not add to the competitive pressures of modern parenting. If they don't have anything at all to say, they don't use Fakebook to say it. And they never, ever complain about the temperature of the Moet in a first-class airport lounge.

Stop the sharenting

As always, kids are at the heart of this obsessive brand of parenting. Hyper-parents don't just post endlessly about their fabulous lives, but document every blink, yawn and gurgle from their offspring. It's called sharenting. A child isn't a valuable new member of their family so much as a content provider for social media. One woman on kidspot.com.au thought her new mum friend made a mistake when she posted 70 photos of her daughter's face on Facebook. It was no accident, according to Nama Winston. The woman was just obsessed with her baby's face and no doubt thought other people should be too.

Some people don't know when to stop. I know that some of my friends are scrunchers rather than folders. I know the intimate details of their unborn baby's fundal height. And I know that one friend's husband farted while watching TV last night and tried to blame the dog.

Sharents will celebrate their baby's first potty performance with a Facebook post – yes, complete with photo and hashtag #pottyqueen. Before their kids are old enough to object – let alone hire a lawyer – they have posted thousands of their most intimate and mundane moments. Their misspelled handwritten Mother's Day cards declaring how much they 'wuv yew'. Their ribbons for being crap but still managing to turn up on sports day. The three out of 20 they got on their grade five maths test. Bless.

The problem for half-arsed parents who just don't care is that it's not just Proud Parent who's guilty of oversharing these days. It's Worried Parent, Paranoid Parent and Hypochondriac Parent.

This is much more of a concern because of the hideous nature of the posts. I'm talking about photos of rashes in intimate areas, weirdly shaped toenails and inexplicably long diatribes about balls not descending in time for the first swimming lesson. One friend of mine even posted pictures of her son's earwax in the hope that someone else would help her diagnose a medical condition.

Many sharents figure they'll stop posting when their memory fills up on their iPhone, which will be in around 2056. In the meantime, they're boring the pants off half-arsed parents who don't behave like this. According to one survey, 72 per cent of parents say online sharing makes them 'feel as if they are not alone'. However, if they keep it up, they soon will be.

It's even worse when the posts show their kids looking silly or embarrassing. My friends share photos of their kids in the bath, totally nude, playing with tampons, failing at potty training and getting stuck in weird places like toilets. One pal of mine recently posted his son's schoolwork that consisted of misspelling the word 'can't', with the 'a' replaced by 'u', and without the apostrophe. Think about that one for a moment. I was faced with this conundrum a few years ago when my young son did some really cute drawings of snails that looked like a man's meat and two veg floating in the sky. I was very tempted to post it. So funny! Think of all the likes on Facebook! Think of all the laughs at school drop-off! But I held myself back, secure in the knowledge that he didn't need his flying penis homework coming back to haunt him when he applies for his first job.

I am not immune to the sharenting bug, as you've probably worked out by this stage. I sometimes even share cute moments online, such as when my younger son drew love hearts for me on my car window in the dirt. I know there are times when I should listen to myself. It is definitely time to stop sharing every second of your damn kids' lives on social media. Remember, no one is as interested as you. No one really cares. You may think they do. They may act as if they do. But they don't. She ate mashed banana: we don't care. He sat up for the first time: we don't care. She used a potty. WE JUST DON'T CARE. Somewhere between a parent's right to free speech and a child's right to privacy is everyone else's right not to be bored. Half-arsed parents know this, and they don't have the time or energy to post endlessly on social media.

There are also the kids to consider, and half-arsed parents don't utter that sentence too often. Kids won't care so much about the re-emergence of photos from that cute period where they loved going to the supermarket in nothing but a superhero cape and gum boots. (I am still not over that phase.) But they might be a bit shitty to discover their flying penises homework pops up on the social media data report of a prospective employer.

It's no wonder kids these days are demanding parents get their permission before posting photos of them online. Teenage girls are the most sensitive, particularly of 'ugly or embarrassing' photos that might not match their own carefully curated social media image, as one study found. Celebrity offspring are not immune from these feelings either, with Apple Martin, daughter of actor and influencer Gwyneth Paltrow, objecting to a photo her mother posted of her while skiing. 'Mom we have discussed this. You may not post anything without my consent,' she said.

Sometimes it's not easy. US writer and lawyer Christie Tate has written about how her daughter asked her to take down all the essays and photos about her, and she refused. She's a mother and didn't think it was fair she couldn't write about raising her kids. She subsequently agreed to give her daughter veto rights on all photos, and to let her know ahead of time what she writes about her. Seems fair. My own kids have read what's written about them here, occasionally trimming or tweaking stories, mostly the ones about poo and toilets.

But let's not go overboard. Some commentators suggest such regular social media posting is tantamount to child abuse; that parents are offering kiddies up to paedophiles on a platter. Others say parents are at risk of violating their children's human rights. In one article, a woman called Apricot, who's 30 and from the UK, talked about her concern about the impact of her social media posts on her daughter. 'How could I instil a principle of privacy when I had essentially devalued hers from the beginning?' she wrote. Half-arsed parents don't do this, not because of the risk of abuse, but because it's pissing off the kids and boring everyone else witless. Half-arsed parents don't know everything, but they do know not to take social media advice from someone called Apricot.

Keep it real

As I mentioned earlier, not all social media influencers are narcissistic goddesses with a full face of make-up on before dawn. Some are funny, real and down-to-earth. Half-arsed parents are more likely to follow US mother-of-two Danielle Bevens, who isn't ashamed to show her son eating pizza in his nappy for breakfast. Bevens talks about her struggle to find clean clothes, her loss of motivation and her to-do list, which reads:

1. Wake up
2. Survive
3. Go back to bed.

One post reads, 'I'm in a dark place right now. Not emotionally. Just that I'm hiding in the cupboard from my kids.' The caption is, 'Isn't dad home yet?' Right on, sister. There's also Hipster Mum, who offers witty real-life memes. 'Mum flu: It's like man flu, but no one gives a sh*t' and 'I hate when I am waiting for mum to cook dinner then I remember I am the mum and I have to cook dinner.'

As someone who's had her fair share of real-life mummy moments, I can identify with this approach much more. I remember the time I asked my younger son, who was about four, for some privacy while I was on the loo. He stepped inside, closed the door and said, 'There, now we can have some privacy. Are you doing a number one or a two?' And there's my daughter, who loves building me up. 'You look like a teenager,' she'll tell me. 'But only from behind, not your face. Definitely not your face.' (For the record, these stories were sanctioned by my kids, and weren't posted on the internet the moment they happened.) Half-arsed parents like this 're-tell' therapy. It's like retail therapy, but cheaper, and no one will make you bench-press toddlers.

Fathers on social media are a kinder and funnier tribe, often swapping self-deprecating dad jokes and husband fails. Whether it's serious sites like The Good Men Project or The Father Hood, or parenting blogs like Dad and Buried or Reservoir Dad, men have found their voices online. Daddy bloggers often provide a perspective that could only come from a man, like this tweet from @WildeThingy: 'Me: I'm starting to worry the babysitter has a crush on me. Wife: *looks me up and down* 'She's reliable. I'll take the risk.' Abe Yospe – who's the @cheesyboy22 guy – also writes a lot about fatherhood. 'The lady at the museum said it would be a 3 hour tour. Yeah right, I saw *Gilligan's Island*. I'm not falling for that,' he tweeted. While such comments play into the hopeless dad stereotype, they transcend it because the bloggers' enthusiasm for their role as fathers, and their affection for their kids, shines through.

Hallelujah for these half-arsed dads. Wish there was more content like it on social media from mums too, like Celeste Barber. Barber has nearly seven million followers on Instagram and recreates the poses adopted by celebrities and models, often drawing attention to her own normal body and shape. She is a deadset half-arsed legend. Her posts make women feel happy and good about themselves. She says motherhood has taught her that 'sleep is overrated and wine becomes your best friend'. As she puts it, 'I feel I'm so bloody satisfied now with kids. When I'm at work, I get really excited that I have the boys to go home to, then when I'm at home with the kids I get REALLY excited that I have to go to work.'

There's no doubt social media is changing the way images are presented and consumed, leading to a redrawing of the boundaries between real and unreal. As Barber told *Stellar* magazine recently, 'Back in the day, we had an understanding that only a handful of people belong in magazines, and they're all photoshopped . . . But now you've got influencers posting something ridiculous and putting the caption as "Just dropping the kids off at school . . ." And [it's] like, "Shut up. That's not normal! Don't sell it like it's an attainable lifestyle when it's not!"' Half-arsed parents only follow those who make them feel good. They can foil a Facebook faker, ignore an Insta-scammer and shun a sharenter. Oh, and you won't ever find them posting 70 near-identical photos of their baby's face on social media.

PART TWO

Half-Arsed How-Tos

Chapter 8

BIRTH, BABIES AND BULLSH*T

By now, I hope you've got the general idea about half-arsed parenting. We like kids enough to have them, but they don't rule our lives. We don't revel in every gurgle, kick and cry. We get on with raising them without posting endlessly on social media because we know no one really cares. In this second part, we'll go through some major milestones to show how half-arsed basics can be applied to each age and stage of parenting. From prams to proms, tots to teens, this is what you need to know.

Pregnancy: what the hell is happening to me?

Remember what it was like to be pregnant? You're 35 weeks and you've gained 25 kg (only 4 kg of which is baby weight). You've got a heat rash that would fry an egg, varicose veins in unmentionable places, and you've discovered that your favourite comfy jeans no longer fit around your burgeoning girth. In fact, you can't even get one leg in. You realise that unless you cut up the curtains *Sound of Music*-style, you have absolutely nothing to wear.

And yet photos of self-satisfied pregnant celebs are everywhere. In ten-page spreads in *Hello!*, Gwyneth/Jennifer/Kate/Miranda/Sienna/Beyoncé gush about how much they *love* being pregnant. They've kept their Grammy/Oscar award-winning careers going, are more in love than EVER and had great fun getting the nursery decorated.

Celebrities like this also have a designer pregnancy wardrobe that allows them to fit into a number of fashion categories like 'cool and casual' (Hilary Duff), 'preppie-chic' (Jennifer Garner) or 'rock-n-roll mama' (Gwen Stefani). It sure beats the $200 eBay nursery splurge and hand-me-down kaftans of most normal pregnant women. Even if a pregnant celebrity is huge, she has a $25,000 Hermes handbag to hide behind. The IKEA blue bags favoured by the time-poor half-arsed parent are never, ever going to look remotely chic, although they will hide the fact that her ankles have disappeared altogether.

Remember Hilaria Baldwin, the wife of actor Alec Baldwin, who obsessively documented each pregnancy one exhibitionist post at a time? It was awful. It might have been different if Baldwin looked like many other pregnant women – 15 kg over their normal weight with reflux and bad hair – but she did not. She was perfect and wanted us to know it. Half-arsed parents know women like this set a false standard for other pregnant women, and give them a wide berth.

Another popular pregnancy blogger was personal trainer Sophie Guidolin, who was 27 weeks pregnant with twins when she posted shots of herself lifting 30 kg weights. There was also Sarah Stage, an underwear model who posted shots showing her stomach's firm muscles when she was about to give birth. Half-arsed parents know that these women are not posting photos of themselves because they want to demystify pregnancy or break down barriers. Rather, it's about showing they can rock a $300 bikini when they're 38 weeks pregnant. We know it's pure narcissism and does nothing to help the rest of us feel good when we appear to be 78 weeks pregnant at the halfway mark.

Half-arsed parents know most of this pregnancy perfection is conjured up for the cameras. Articles about celebrities who are expecting are the very last thing pregnant women should be reading. Ordinary women don't spend their days surrounded by stylists, wear $700 pregnancy jeans or have in-house cooks, cleaners, nannies and personal trainers. Researcher Dr Rachel Gow found that in many of the celebrity pregnancy articles she looked at, weight gain (which is normal and inescapable for most women) is portrayed as negative. And only six per cent of articles suggest the celebrity new mum is dissatisfied with her post-baby body, whereas in real life, 40 per cent of women are unhappy with their weight after giving birth.

Even harder to stomach (literally) are pregnant celebrities like actor Eva Longoria who acknowledge they put on weight and have heartburn but still go on about how #blessed they feel. Longoria says, 'you have to thank your body for creating life.

You have to have gratitude towards your body and that's how I approached it. From the heartburn to the weight gain, I loved everything that happened as it was the product of my son growing.' Yeah, I get it and I am happy for her. But expecting gratitude from a pregnant woman who hasn't seen her private parts without a mirror for eight months, and whose bikini line is threatening to cross state borders unaccompanied, may be expecting a bit too much.

TV star Kim Kardashian took a different approach. Forget gratitude. With her, it was glamour all the way. She was seen as a sexy jezebel because she refused to change the way she dressed and behaved when she was pregnant. She dressed that bump in spandex, lace, Lycra and shiny black leather – often all in one outfit. Well, what else would you expect from someone who said that if she were a man for a day, she'd want to have sex with herself? When Kardashian got pre-eclampsia when pregnant with her daughter North, she put it down to God 'teaching her a lesson' for 'thinking she's so hot'. Half-arsed women don't want to have to be sexy when they're pregnant. Feeling sexy got them in this situation, so it's hardly going to do them much good now. Even so, Kardashian didn't deserve to have photos of her wearing a black and white dress while pregnant posted online next to photos of a black and white whale with the caption, 'Who wore it best?'.

Half-arsed pregnant mums do their best, confident in the knowledge no one expects much anyway. We get by, we make do, we get on with it. The half-arsed pregnant woman doesn't try to be a fashion model in the latest trends; she's more likely to get by with a rubber band keeping her jeans done up. If she's got any concerns, she shares them with her partner, parent, GP, health nurse or best friend, not her Instagram followers. There are good days – the first kick! – and days when she's so tired she can barely lift a hairbrush, let alone cook dinner.

Half-arsed women do not have the time or energy to document or debate every aspect of their pregnancy, and wish more women felt the same way. They don't pose for pregnancy glamour shots, have plaster casts made of their bare bellies to hang on the wall or have loud conversations at work about how bad their constipation has been since the second trimester. They will not post photos of the blue line on the wee stick or share their 3-D ultrasound images set to whale music. And they know no one except their immediate family cares about their birth plan. 'Gee, can't wait to hear about the innovative squatting position you've chosen for labour,' said no co-worker ever.

Birth: get this thing out of me

After pregnancy, there's the birth to worry about. Most women are too concerned about how they are going to pass a basketball through their lady bits to worry about what the next 18 years of parenting will hold. It's probably a good thing they're not ready to consider the moment, 14 years later, when their child will thrust 'dem pits' in their face and ask them to inhale. They've had 40 excruciating weeks to ponder all the birthing options they will be judged on. Caesar or no caesar? Natural or epidural? Induced or at-term? Public or private? Hospital or birthing centre? Which gynaecologist? Which midwife? Which of my many lovers did this to me? (Just kidding about the last one.)

It hasn't always been like this. Forty-nine years ago, my mother gave birth to me in Tamworth. She and my dad were visiting their parents with my sister. They were on the road halfway between Sydney and Brisbane when my mother went into labour six weeks early in a motel. Mum was rushed to hospital, where the staff made it very clear there was no role for Dad to play at that end of proceedings. His job was done nine months earlier. He took my sister, who was a toddler, back to the motel and celebrated my birth some hours later by giving her a sip of the froth from his beer. It was the 70s, so it's possible he also let her light him a Marlboro Red and drive the Kingswood as well.

My mother lay flat on her back, was given drugs and had me a few hours later. I was premmie so went into a humidicrib for a month or so. Did my parents drop everything to be by my bedside? No! They flew back home to Western Australia with my sister, and my Gran flew up from Sydney to be with me. There were no grand birth announcements, no coy little social media stunts, no graphic birthing videos, no placenta recipes and no brealfies (breastfeeding selfies). Half-arsed parents approve of this back-to-basics approach.

Half-arsed new parents like modern conveniences like drugs, epidurals and grandparents who love babysitting. They're too tired to sugar-coat the truth and you won't find them posing in ball gowns with their newborns, especially if the babies don't have nappies on. Take a recent photoshoot with model Rachael Finch. Four weeks after giving birth, Finch was photographed cradling her naked newborn and wearing a floaty chiffon dress while sitting on a calico painter's sheet strewn with strangely leafless hydrangeas. 'It feels so perfect to have a boy and a girl,' Finch gushes in the story. She also reveals her husband would breastfeed if he could, and is her rock and saviour. Yes, because of course he is. Hasn't she worked out by now that bare baby bums and ball gowns don't mix?

The same interview reveals Finch drinks milk-free lattes (huh?) and was exercising two days after giving birth. Two days after giving birth, I was still high on drugs. Four weeks later, I even managed to brush my hair *and* my teeth before I left the house.

I prefer the post-birth story from Laura Byrne, partner of radio host and former Bachelor Matty J. 'I was in labour and I didn't get a break. It was constant contractions. So after about an hour I was like, fuck this, give me the drugs . . . I was so off my rocket.' All hail, Laura, you half-arsed hero.

Birthing trends to avoid like the plague

Gender reveal

These days, handing around a photo of a grainy ultrasound with the relevant bits circled in texta doesn't cut it. People throw parties with games and cakes in order to reveal the gender of their child. It's not the half-arsed parenting way, that's for sure. You won't see me expecting friends and family to set aside five hours to celebrate the sex of my unborn offspring. There has also been a recent spate of gender reveals based around coloured smoke. This can be risky, as some parents-to-be found out, when their car caught fire doing a burnout at a baby shower in country Victoria. The burnout was the gender reveal: the smoke was pink. No doubt they were inspired by a gender reveal party in Arizona that caused a bushfire which spread over 47,000 acres and cost US$11 million. The fire raged for six days and took 800 fire fighters to contain. I'll bet the dad-to-be wished he'd bought a doodle cake instead. (Yes, sadly, this is a thing.)

Crowd birthing

The half-arsed mother in labour also does not need an audience while she is on all fours, screaming like an animal. She does not subscribe to the 'crowd birthing' movement that offers an entourage for the final reveal. It's a birth, not a reality TV show. She is also smart enough not to try free birthing or hypno-birthing unless it's in a hospital or birthing centre. If pushed, the only weirdo birth trend she'd be willing to try is the one from 18th-century France, where newborns were bathed in wine. The half-arsed mother will also avoid an orgasmic birth. If she's like most women, it's been a full nine months since she was orgasmic and it is the last thing on her mind. Nor will she have a Lotus birth, which involves leaving the umbilical cord and placenta attached until they shrivel up and drop off naturally. Some say carrying around the placenta is a breeding ground for infection. Others say it makes a handy bag. As my younger son would say: No. Just. No.

Siblings in the labour ward

A few years ago, celebrity chef Jamie Oliver and his wife Jools revealed their two older daughters, Poppy Honey and Daisy Boo, witnessed the birth of their brother and cut the cord.

Eeww. One generation ago, even fathers weren't allowed in maternity wards, let alone siblings running loose with scalpels. *The Big Bang Theory*'s Mayim Bialik let her two-year-old son sit in a highchair and eat muesli while she was in labour at home with her second child. For the record, he was prepared for the ordeal by watching birthing videos. (Either that or the shower scene in *Psycho*.) 'He got freaked out by the blood, but it was still nice,' Bialik says. Cue 30 years of therapy. Half-arsed parents don't agree families and other siblings have a major role to play in the labour process. They think the best place for siblings during birth is Grandma and Grandpa's house, or anywhere someone will pay them attention.

Social media updates

Nor will half-arsed parents be offering live-streaming from the maternity ward or updates with real-time contraction information. They are smart enough to know no one else cares about what's going on until the little bugger's safely arrived. Nor will they follow another trend and share photos of the baby before he or she has been cleaned up and had the cord cut. In half-arsed parents' photos, you can be guaranteed no vagina shots, no bloody bits and no newborn covered in vernix (the waxy white stuff). The half-arsed new mother will accept push presents in the form of jewellery, dinner vouchers or spa treatments, but not bags of Huggies or manual breast pumps. Kylie Jenner got a new Ferrari, but most new mums would settle for a 12-month Netflix membership and noise-cancelling headphones.

Breastfeeding porn

Half-arsed mums try to breastfeed because it's best for the baby, free and you don't have to wash bottles at 3 am. However, they don't beat themselves up about it if they can't, and don't judge others if they can't either. You won't find half-arsed mums joining the breastfeeding selfie craze, which involves women posting revealing shots of themselves while their bubs are feeding. Remember Russian supermodel Natalia Vodianova, who posted an arty black-and-white photo of herself naked and reclining, staring seductively at the camera while the baby got busy at the boob? It's not about the baby; it's a case of *Look at me! See? I'm hot, even when breastfeeding*. It's not empowering, it's ridiculous.

Aussie supermodel Miranda Kerr posted similar shots, using photos of her breastfeeding to share her eternal maternal bliss with the world. This might be 'just another day in the office' – as Kerr described it – but there aren't too many women who will identify with her prettily posed workplace snap. Kerr even makes breastfeeding look downright sexy, which is something that few women will identify with. Breastfeeding doesn't come easily to everyone. It's rewarding, but it can be bloody hard work. Having Miranda boasting about how it's the 'most natural thing in the world' alienates women who are struggling to get it right. With three kids, I've done a fair bit of breastfeeding over the years, sometimes when working, and I've never looked the least bit like a supermodel, Russian or otherwise.

The half-arsed mum is also unlikely to post shots of herself breastfeeding on one of the many Facebook groups set up to celebrate ordinary women. These include not only tiny bubs sucking away but pre-schoolers grabbing a feed from mum, and even a naked woman doing an upside-down yoga pose with a toddler popping over for a snack. I loved my breastfeeding body (I never had such a great rack in my life) but I am certainly not rushing to post pics of my bub suckling at my breasts. Half-arsed mums think breastfeeding is important, but they don't think people need to see photographic evidence that their nipples are now the size of saucers.

Half-arsed parents are also unlikely to be proponents of extreme breastfeeding. I'll never forget the sight of a friend's neighbour – a breastfeeding activist – feeding her four-year-old son. He casually walked up to her at a barbecue, lifted her top and attached himself in front of everyone. He had a drink then walked away. No one knew where to look, but the mum barely registered his presence and carried on talking like nothing was happening. While this is something kids might do at home, it didn't seem appropriate on a play date. Rather than break down barriers, extreme breastfeeding has the opposite effect. It turns people off, and fuels the misconception that mothers lack the appropriate discretion for breastfeeding in public.

It's a pity, because Australia's breastfeeding rates are way lower than they should be. Just 14 per cent of women breastfeed to one year, and only 25 per cent breastfeed exclusively to six months, which is recommended. I know I am not going to win any natural mothering awards here, but maybe it's time to stop when kids are old enough to walk up and ask for a breastfeed. Half-arsed parents are more likely to give their four-year-old a sandwich when they're hungry, not a suck on a nipple that's now almost reaching the ground.

Sleeping through and other BS

We need to remember how hard it is to be parents the first time around – it's one of the best forms of contraception. It's tough. Not only are you trying to work out how to get a onesie done up without the baby rolling off the change table, but also how to block out annoying relatives who say things like, 'Oh, you're going back to work? I thought you loved your baby.'

Sharing the housework is an important part of the half-arsed manifesto. One Victorian study found depression and anxiety among new mums were reduced by a third when they were given help to soothe their crying babies and retrain housework-shy husbands. The Monash University 'What Were We Thinking?' trial involved women, partners and babies attending a one-day seminar on topics such as soothing the baby, negotiating household chores and encouraging each other rather than criticising.

It's a major issue because traditional roles still dominate. Dads are usually first to go back to work. On average, Australian men take only two weeks of paid parental leave, although many would like much more time off than that. This leaves it up to mums to work out how to look after a screaming ball of red flesh who wakes up every 21.6 minutes. Eighteen months down the track, it's no wonder most are exhausted. Studies show mums with new bubs do a 'fourth shift' at night, losing more than five hours of sleep a week compared to those who do not have kids. New fathers miss two hours of sleep and have much better-quality slumber.

Half-arsed parents know they will be quizzed three hours after giving birth about whether their baby is 'sleeping through'. It's always offered as an innocent question, but don't be fooled. It's the ultimate measure of the ability of new parents and the number one topic parents lie to each other about. (Other top-five parenting whoppers are nits, sickness, yelling and kids' milestones.)

Half-arsed parents know one important fact: people's definition of what it means to 'sleep through' varies by as much as five hours a night. Some parents expect nothing less than ten hours uninterrupted sleep a night. Others say a baby 'sleeps through' when he or she sleeps from midnight to 5 am, according to a New Zealand study of 412 mothers with children under two.

It's no wonder researchers are calling for a new parent-based definition of sleeping through that sets a common standard.

Half-arsed parents are realistic in what they expect babies to do, and don't feel like failures if their bub is not 'sleeping through' at four weeks. I have three kids, so I know first-hand how sleep-deprivation gnaws at the core of your soul and reduces the smartest, brightest person to a blithering mess. Throw in a bright-eyed friend whose six-week-old is already 'sleeping through', and you've got a crisis on your hands. Half-arsed parents muddle through by accepting that broken sleep is part of the deal. For me, this worked much better than trying to teach my first baby to sleep through when he clearly wasn't ready to do so. I am happy to claim success with my first son in this area. He's now a teenager and I have trouble waking him up.

When you're feeling worried, remember that Australian babies are among the world's best sleepers. One study of 2154 infants from birth to age three found our babies and toddlers are generally in bed by 7.35 pm and wake once a night for 23 minutes. Only seven per cent share a bed with mum or dad. Experts say these results are commendable, with Australian babies getting up to an hour more sleep a night than babies from Asia and Europe. And yet one-third of parents are worried their baby has a sleep problem.

The half-arsed mother doesn't try to be a hero. After the birth, she knows she needs someone to pop over, put on a load of washing, unpack the dishwasher and tell her it's going to be okay. She's also smart enough to watch *Blankety Blanks* or *Melrose Place* reruns at 3 am rather than check her social media feed. She's leaking from both nipples, can't get the baby to attach, hasn't had a shower in three days and the toddler has watched so much TV, he thinks he *is* Fireman Sam. The last thing she needs are friends on Insta boasting about how their newborn is already sleeping through (#perfectioninbabyform) while her son is pretending to put out fires in the corner of the living room with the watering can. Toddlers. Don't get me started . . .

Chapter 9

TODDLERS: HOW LOW CAN YOU GO?

Half-arsed parents know raising toddlers is ten per cent fabulous and 90 per cent slog. They take it easy if they can. They accept help and let go of judgment, good taste and stain-free clothing. No one can deny the cuteness overload that comes from watching ankle-biters stomp around in their father's shoes or cover themselves in spaghetti at dinner. But it does wear off after lengthy exposure – and the stress of 53 loads of washing a week. Yep, toddlers are cute; they have to be, or they wouldn't survive long enough to inflict their own offspring on their parents.

Author Bunmi Laditan has it all worked out. Her book *The Honest Toddler: Not Potty Trained. Not Trying* is brilliant. The honest toddler does his best to prevent siblings by making sure his parents never have time alone to have sex, thinks naps are for wimps, and willingly ignores any parental request unless it involves a river of juice. The book, written in the voice of a two-year-old, has lines like, 'When you shower alone, you hurt your toddler's feelings and damage her spirit,' and 'Toddlers are tired of hearing Facebook notifications during story time.'

From January Jones finding Lego in the toilet to Snooki doing selfies with a prostrate toddler on the bathroom floor in the background, celebs are a bit more down to earth during the toddler phase. *How I Met Your Mother* star Alyson Hannigan asks, 'why don't kids understand their nap time is not for them but for us?' Actor Olivia Wilde posts about her messy hair days. 'I call this hairstyle, "keep the kid alive". Products you'll need: sweat, string cheese, diaper rash cream, chewed-up crayon, snot, and an enthusiastic spritz of panic.' Funny. Singer Carrie Underwood says, 'It just occurred to me that the majority of my diet is made up of foods my kid didn't finish.' Sounds familiar. Famous dads like Chris Pratt, Ryan Reynolds and David Beckham are in on the action, posting about being called fat, given psychoanalysis by their kids and getting grief from their toddlers on planes. Singer Justin Timberlake even admits to getting peed on. Half-arsed parents draw strength from these tales.

My kids were quite sweet as toddlers. My daughter used to hook her arm around my neck when I'd lie next to her in her little white bed, murmuring, 'Mummy, *my* mummy' in contented tones. She begged me to 'be happy' when I was sad, and gave me big sloppy wet kisses to 'make it better'. I was her best friend and her greatest enemy – and that was in the five minutes before bedtime. She used to think the sight of my naked body was particularly hilarious and had an obsession with watching me in the toilet, providing a running commentary on the action. 'Mummy did poos,' she would solemnly announce to shop assistants. 'Not just wees today, poos as well.'

In *You Will (Probably) Survive*, Lauren Dubois perfectly captures what she calls 'the crapshow that is negotiating with your megalomaniacal toddler'. She kicks off a chapter titled 'Toddlers are the Worst' by imagining toddler behaviour performed by 52-year-olds. 'You and Barb are going shopping. Barb would like to go shopping in the nude. You look at Barb, boobs hanging to her waist and explain she will have to wear clothes to the shops. She kicks you in the chin and runs away.' Yep, we've all been there. As Dubois explains, 'No matter how many times you tell yourself that your child is only two years old and you are an adult who should be able to keep a steady head, it won't make it any easier to deal with your little pest . . . We know you love your child. That's never been in question. But, darl, sometimes it's impossible to like them.' Oh yes, I know exactly what she means.

Half-arsed parents survive by working out how far their standards can drop while keeping them safe long enough so they can fund their old age.

No bare bums or fighting

A few years ago, one UK mother took to popular website mumsnet to ask advice from others on this issue. It prompted a vigorous debate about where to draw the line when it comes to pre-schoolers' behaviour. A dad called Saucy Jack offered his assessment. 'No biting the cat. No putting things up your bottom.

No throwing things at the telly.' Brilliant. I've had three kids, and not one of them has ever put foreign objects up their bottom (as far as I know). But my three-year-old daughter did lie on the floor of a fancy shoe shop waving her legs in the air, and showing off her bottom while yelling, 'botterm, botterm'. She's now a teenager and I hope she doesn't draw inspiration from that moment once she starts dating.

Another mumsnet mum revealed she draws the line at 'bare bums or fighting. That's it.' If only adults would stick to the same rules. Parents on the site thought it was adorable when toddlers would tell smokers they're going to die, tell family members they are fat and advise strangers that 'drinking makes mummy happy'. One talked about the 'cute' things her daughter did, such as drinking from the dogs' water bowl and blowing bubbles in their potty with a straw. Clearly, some parents have very strange ideas about where to draw the line.

When my older son was a toddler, I never knew if I was too hard on him or not hard enough. Line? What line? My policy of choosing my battles meant I made a big deal about him holding my hand when crossing roads, but I let him make a mess and wear what he wanted. I didn't ever feel like I got that balance right, which is why he was often at the shops in mismatched gumboots, Batman cape and a tutu covered in jam stains. Same thing for my younger son. When he was a toddler, he loved to pick weeds for me from other people's gardens, took forever to get in and out of a car seat and always left the house with a little collection of irreplaceable Lego, which was usually lost.

Half-arsed parents work out for themselves where to draw the line without taking advice from nosy in-laws, opinionated friends or Insta influencers. In the end, I indulged the Lego because it was cute, but I did start backing out of the driveway in a bid to get him to buckle up faster. And although I enjoyed the flower picking, I didn't always have time for him to choose the perfect yellow flower from a field of 500 other identical weeds on every nature strip on the way to school. Yes, I did tell him to hurry and pretend to walk off and leave him behind. Half-arsed parents figure out whatever works and keeps them sane and go with it.

It's not easy. Oh Lordy, no. As a toddler, my older son was so contrary that he instinctively craved whatever he knew I didn't want him to have.

'No whining,' I told him one day. 'Me want whining, me want whining,' he screamed immediately, not even knowing what whining was. He's now a teenager and sounds like a man when he speaks – usually to ask for money. When I ask him to get off his phone when I am driving him places, he looks at me sadly. 'That's right Mum, you're not a millennial, you're no good at multitasking,' he says. Clearly, I still don't know where to draw the line.

Don't give them too much

These days, toddlers are as over-protected and over-indulged as older kids. Experts say parents should give kids space to practise and manage their emotions independently, only guiding them when they need it. But hyper-parents try to dominate their kids' lives, even showing them how to play. It's not good for them or the kids. Dr Nicole Perry from the University of Minnesota found overcontrolling parenting at age two led to poor emotional regulation at age five, which led to emotional issues at school and less academic productivity at age ten. And – presumably – becoming needy narcissists at age 20.

Hyper-parents also shower their kids with endless presents and toys, ignoring the evidence that kids do better with fewer things to play with. One study found toddlers with four toys played for longer and were less distracted than those with 16 toys. Isn't that amazing? Funnily enough, her study didn't look at the impact of the 250 toys owned by the average Australian child.

Less screen time can also be good for toddlers, with a lot of evidence showing kids and parents who are on screens for many hours a day have impaired conversation and social skills. And yet you'll never see me suggesting parents should take screens off toddlers altogether. What do you think I am, a sadist? Half-arsed parents do what they need to do to get through the day; usually this means a bit of screen time, then a play. They value their own sanity too much to come between a toddler and an iPad at 5 pm.

Researchers also say a good chat with toddlers goes a long way – ten years or more in fact. Toddlers with parents who spend lots of time listening and chatting with them are more likely to have better language skills and higher IQs. Of course, it's important to watch what you say around the little rug-rats. Lauren Dubois found this out the hard way. 'All those times you thought it was okay to swear in front of a six-month-old haunt you as your child waltzes into childcare and sings merrily to her teachers, 'Good morning, bitches'. Imagine that.

Re-peeling bananas and other tantrum-inducers

Dr Monique Robinson from the Telethon Kids Institute says 90 per cent of kids have tantrums between the age of one and four. Tantrums peak at two, when 'the perfect storm' of a developing sense of independence and desire for autonomy collides with the inability to express themselves verbally. Robinson says tantrums happen when a child wants something they can't have, wants to avoid something, wants attention or if they are hungry, tired, unwell or frustrated. That's most toddlers, most of the time. The littlest things set my first son off when he was a toddler. He used to have a screaming fit, demanding that I reattach grapes that I'd plucked off the stems and placed in a bowl. 'Mines,' he'd say petulantly, grabbing the bowl. 'Me do it! Meeeee doooo iiiiit.'

He'd then throw himself on the floor and cry uncontrollably. How could I explain that the grapes won't go back on? Or that you can't re-peel bananas? I spent years taking deep breaths and trying to control my urge to walk out the front door and not come back. I wrote a piece about this time of my life and submitted it to a local magazine. It was rejected by the editor as he told me it was too negative and 'didn't capture the magic of parenthood'. Magic? There's nothing magic about life with toddlers. It's a dog-eat-dog time of survival. The only magic comes from knowing that if you hang in there long enough, this stage will pass, like the Lego they ate for breakfast.

Half-arsed parents know kids sometimes have tantrums and don't beat themselves up about it. Rather than listen to disapproving outsiders tell them off, they'll stay sane by going to the blog 'Reasons my kid is crying'. Reasons my kid is crying include 'I wouldn't let him keep eating dirt', 'I wouldn't let her wipe my butt' and 'I told him he couldn't take an unwrapped tampon with him to run errands'. The list also includes parents who wanted to put used nappies in the bin, those who failed to make food whole again after a bite had been taken and those who stopped their toddler from using the toilet-cleaning sponge for a face washer. 'I broke his cheese in half', 'He doesn't want the banana he wasn't offered' and 'I wouldn't let him wear his dirty underwear as a hat' are other hilarious reasons for epic meltdowns.

Half-arsed parents toddler-proof their house and do their best to avoid situations where tantrums are likely to happen, such as taking kids to the supermarket when they're tired and hungry. My daughter is now a teenager and I still employ this rule. Rather than taking toddler misbehaviour to heart and blaming themselves, they find routines and short-cuts that make things easier. For me, it was buying half a stick of kabana when I first got to the supermarket, opening it up while I was shopping and letting the kids munch on the fat-injected processed meat by-product while I trawled the aisles. It's not really food but at least it kept them quiet. I also used to feed my first son in the bath as a way to streamline the evening routine. I still remember pushing the little bits of meat sauce through the plug hole as the water drained out.

Dr Robinson says the best way to deal with tantrums is to avoid them. If you're in public, try to redirect their attention. If not, keep calm and get the hell out of there as fast as you can.

We're all in this together

I remember one almighty tantrum my first son had more than a decade ago. We were at a shopping centre and he didn't want to leave the crappy temporary playground set up in the dingy basement food court. I had his newborn sister in a sling wrapped to me. When I tried to drag him off the little slide, he threw himself on the ground and wouldn't stop screaming and kicking. When I tried to get him back in the pram, he started kicking me, which made his sister scream. With her on me, I couldn't physically force him into the pram because I was worried he might hurt her. I was tired and overly sensitive to all eyes that turned my way. Before long, I was crying too. Luckily, a few other mums worked out what was going on and came over to help. Soon, I had a protective circle of helpers around me. I unstrapped my daughter and handed her to a complete stranger to hold while I picked my son up off the floor and physically forced him into the pram. Someone held my handbag. Another watched the pram and my shopping bags. Only with these ladies' help did I manage to get my still-crying daughter back into the sling before leaving, tears still streaming down my face. I've never pushed a pram faster in my life and it took me years to return to the same centre.

The lesson? If you see a mother or father struggling in public, offer practical assistance, not advice or judgment. Hold the bag. Hold the baby. Watch the pram. Block her (or him) so others can't see them crying. Half-arsed parents know that we're all in this together. They care rather than compete. By the way, my son is now a terrific footballer – all that kicking as a toddler must have paid off.

Half-arsed parents don't have all the answers, and don't pretend to. Once when my daughter was one, I found her having a breakfast of used ear cleaners from the bathroom bin, so who are you to take advice about toddlers from me? Get through the day, keep the cap on the gin bottle until 5 pm, and muster the strength to do it all again tomorrow. And if you find a way to reattach grapes, let me know, will you?

Chapter 10

TOO COOL
FOR SCHOOL

Before half-arsed parents know it, their kids are at school and they're thrown into a world of lunchboxes, school websites (which they will never remember the password for) and the dreaded demands of homework. There's nothing worse than your child remembering on a Sunday night they have to make a solar-powered engine with little more than five pipe cleaners, a bit of spit and an old car battery. And don't get me started on book and stationery lists. These days, a few chewed-up pencils and a couple of blue Bics don't cut it. Nothing less than a Textsurfer highlighter, Colourhide binder and UHU Magic Blu Glu Stic will do. From now on, I am going to blame UHU for my kids' atrocious spelling.

Schools don't just assess kids. They are also good at handing out tests of parental endurance and intelligence. It's not fun. A friend recently had to make her son a French hat out of only recycled materials for a 14 July parade. Despite her child only remembering on the morning of the event, she fashioned a wonky tricorn out of yesterday's sports pages in 15 seconds flat. Her son assessed her creation with cool, cruel eyes and said, 'I'm going to have the shittiest French hat in the class'. Direct quote from her five-year-old.

It doesn't help that schools today are minefields of political correctness. At some places, kids are the bosses and teachers are too scared of being sued to do their job effectively. Discipline is just about non-existent. One relief teacher told me she was not able to tell off a child who talked back to her. She was told, 'we don't do that sort of thing here'. Educators are expected to be quasi-parents, responsible for the moral and emotional growth of the students. Kids are so anxious and over-protected they're taught four new Rs: resilience, rights and respectful relationships, rather than reading, writing and 'rithmetic. Students are given catastrophe training, emotional literacy lessons and encouraged to show random acts of kindness to each other. At one primary school, kids act out what it looks like to be happy, sad or anxious in a bid to teach them to recognise their emotions. Since when did kids have to be taught things like this, rather than learn it as part of growing up?

Making things harder are a group of litigious parents standing by to sue schools for what most would consider the rough and tumble of childhood. One state has seen a tripling in cases of parents suing the Education Department, with payouts soaring past $7 million in three years. Common sense goes out the window as anxious, guilty parents ring the lawyers instead of the principal the minute something goes wrong. In their eyes, it's not an accident, it's criminal negligence. It's not a mistake, it's a legal failure to take due care. It's not an illness, it's medical malpractice. In this country, schools are worried about being sued for giving students poor grades, for not having enough shade in the playground, for providing computers that might be used for bullying and for having steps the students might fall down. In one case, a prestigious private school was sued because a student didn't get into her preferred law course at a top university. In another, the parents of a student who ran into a wall while playing chasey sued the school. The lawyer father claimed the rules of the game weren't spelled out clearly enough, putting his son at risk.

Half-arsed parents can't be bothered to make a fuss unless it's absolutely necessary. And they sure as hell won't make another newspaper hat because the first one was thought to be shit.

Homework: it's for the kids

Homework is another major battleground between parents and kids. No one can accuse me of doing my kids' homework for them. Even when they were in primary school, they were way ahead of me. The last time I tried, I wasn't much good to them at all. A trapezium is something an acrobat swings on, right? Half-arsed parents help where needed (if they can) but they generally have an approach that's considered innovative and unique in some circles. They think homework is for kids to learn, not for parents to show off. They will not be one of those parents who march proudly through the school gate carrying their child's science project for them. The assignment was one planet, but they've done all eight in a 3-D model that is so large it had to be ferried in a mini-bus.

Psychologist Dr Locke did a study involving 886 parents of children in prep to year 12 and found a correlation between overparenting and the willingness of parents to do their kids' homework. Not surprisingly, she concluded that 'extreme efforts by parents to promote academic achievement could be undermining the development of independent and resilient performance in their children'. Overprotective parents spend a lot of time doing their kids' homework, fuelled by the belief that the kid won't do it well enough. Half-arsed parents are not falling for this. Don't forget, if you're having problems getting your kids to do homework, ask them to help out around the house. It's amazing how they suddenly remember they've got maths revision to do when you ask them to dry the dishes.

School reports get a J for Jargon

Half-arsed parents also don't like the trend for complicated new-age jargon used in many school reports. One preschool report I saw recently noted that the four-year-old boy liked new challenges, dressing up and gardening. This was useful information. But it also said he was good at 'demonstrating an increased knowledge and respect for the natural and constructed environments' and 'engages in enjoyable, reciprocal interactions using verbal and non-verbal language'. Whaaat? All half-arsed parents want to know is that their kid is no longer eating glue at snack time, has stopped hitting Jimmy in the library corner and can count to ten.

Half-arsed parents want reports to be plain and informative, not artistic creations resembling Aboriginal dot paintings. The school reports my kids got in primary school were very attractive to look at, with good use of light and shade and a range of dots scattered across the landscape. However, they were largely indecipherable to anyone without insider knowledge. Each subject was marked with a white dot for last report's standard, a black dot for progress this year, shading for the expected level and a jagged line to show the child's progress.

Half-arsed parents think As, Bs, Cs and Ds are more useful, particularly because so much of what's written in school reports is baffling. What does it mean for a seven-year-old to be 'consolidating his mathematical principles'? As a parent I need to know if my son can add and subtract. Can he multiply? In short, can he count well enough to realise his brother and sister occasionally raid his tooth-fairy-money tin? Does he know enough to work out that his mother's age and birth date don't match up? And can he work out if he has enough pocket money left over at the end of the week to lend me some?

Deciphering report cards can be an education in itself.

They say: *Your child is an enthusiastic and exuberant member of the class keen to share her knowledge with others.*
They mean: She is an annoying, noisy know-it-all who won't shut up.

They say: *He has a deep understanding of the topic and an excellent recall of facts.*

They mean: I wish he'd stop correcting me in class.

They say: *She can be strong-willed and passionate about her ideas.*

They mean: She's the reason I'm retiring at the end of the year.

Home schooling

Half-arsed parents hope they never have to do home schooling again. Forced on many during Covid, remote learning gave parents a renewed appreciation for how underpaid and underappreciated teachers are. Half-arsed parents spent the whole time wishing kids could go back to school so they could stop pretending to know the capital of Bolivia and the value of pi. (I know the value of pie – does that count?)

In the beginning, I thought home schooling would be easy. There would be nourishing food breaks, family-based exercise pep-ups and a calming, enriching environment. Yeah, right. Things started unravelling at about 9.05 am on day one when we couldn't find the learning tasks on the school's website. Just as I was about to sack myself as the teacher and bring wine o'clock forward by nine hours, I worked out we were using the wrong log-in. Half an hour later my son was googling 'When is school going back?'. No doubt he was frustrated by my high hopes, low standards and inability to do his year five maths homework.

By day two I was thinking of forming a union called the Teacher Appreciation Association of Australia. By day three I went on strike in my bedroom with the Netflix remote and all the kids' leftover Easter eggs. *The Washington Post* told me home schooling was setting back an entire generation of kids. No one seemed to be keeping track of how much it was setting back the parents who were supposed to be supervising them.

Half-arsed parents refused to follow the crowd during home schooling, and stopped taking advice from others about quality family time, mindful check-ins and calming spaces. Instead, they set their own rules. You know, helpful rules, like making sure there were no wine bottles in the background of the Zoom chats with teachers. On occasion they did the kids' work for them and then let them watch TV for the rest of the day so they could get their own work done. And half-arsed parents locked themselves in the bathroom when they needed a break or to make a work call – anywhere from ten minutes to three hours. To stay sane they followed all the #homeschooling fails doing the rounds on social media. One kid wrote in his school diary: 'It is not going good. My mum's getting stressed out. My mum is really getting confused. We took a break so my mum can figure this stuff out and I'm telling you it is not going good.' Half-arsed parents did the bare minimum and didn't sweat the small stuff – in fact, we didn't sweat at all during isolation unless playing a particularly vigorous game of iPad Pong.

During home schooling my 11-year-old flatly refused to do any of the 'random stuff' I had found for him to fill in the day after he'd finished the two hours of work assigned. Instead, he watched *Good Morning Vietnam* at top volume while eating packet pasta, and then kicked the ball against the house for what seemed like an eternity. Well, that's history, PE and home economics taken care of. Nailed it! Half-arsed parents didn't worry if kids didn't learn much and didn't care that it was not 'going good' all the time. But they did pay attention to one important thing: they made sure the computer microphone was off when someone was having a meltdown (especially if it was them).

Parent–teacher interviews: sharing the blame

There's only one thing worse than indecipherable school reports and that's parent–teacher interviews, which are like speed dating but with less chance of a happy ending. At my daughter's school, you're allocated five minutes per teacher and a bell goes when your time is up. The bookings are all electronic, which means you need a degree in IT (or a ten-year-old helper) to get the times you want. It's bloody hard work. I've had more luck booking tickets online to see the Rolling Stones than getting a 3.45 pm appointment with my son's maths teacher on a Thursday.

Booking the interview is only half the battle. Then you have to find the room, work out what teacher you're meant to be seeing and remember what subject they teach. If you're anything like me, you've left work early and rushed to get to room B 48-AK, which is at the opposite end of the school than you thought.

You didn't print out the Excel spreadsheet detailing where you need to be, so you are late, disorganised and hangry. You are just happy getting there on time (sort of) on the right day without your skirt tucked in your undies at the back. Finding out how your daughter is responding to the third semester trigonometry module is way down your list of priorities – which, by 5.35 pm, has a pizza and glass of red as numbers one and two.

Instead, you have to sit with your generous arse perched on a kiddie-sized chair, listening with a straight face as the teacher describes someone you don't even vaguely recognise as your own child. You'll tell the teacher your kid is really enjoying their subject (hoping they don't ask for any evidence of this bald-faced lie). They'll tell you your kid is enjoyable to teach (hoping you can't tell they've already bribed the principal to make sure they don't get them next year).

By the time you get to the good stuff – usually the faults of other children – the bell rings and it's time to move on. Sometimes you get a jargon nerd who doesn't so much converse as deploy a sequence of random phrases. Run a mile if you get one telling you how much they're enjoying the opportunity to interface in your son's developmental space or that he's doing well acquiring the EAPE skills he needs for the SOL and the MAP.

Just when you think you've got away with not being as involved in your child's learning as you should be, the teachers start quizzing you. You don't want to admit you didn't even realise your child was in year eight, let alone learning geography. So you have no chance of being across the fact that they're learning about natural disasters in the Neolithic age.

Half-arsed parents find such interviews are an exercise in humiliation dressed up as an exchange of useful information. Sometimes there's an unspoken mutual understanding: half-arsed parents are happy not to believe everything the child says happens at school if the teacher doesn't believe everything the child says happens at home. As they say on *The Simpsons*: 'Parent–Teacher Night. Let's Share the Blame.'

Painful parents: are you in this list?

School days offer mums and dads another prime opportunity for one-upmanship and oversharing. For some parents, this means getting in the way of teachers who are just doing their job or standing up for their kid even though their kid is the bully. They put low demands on their children to cope when life is not going their way and compensate by putting high demands on other people and institutions. Dr Locke says such parents have 'typically high expectations of the school delivering positive outcomes to the child'. They are also major pains in the arse.

Psychologists interviewed by Dr Locke told of parents constantly badgering the school, running campaigns to decide what class they should be in, confronting teachers about their child's grades or homework and making excuses for their lack of effort. These parental pariahs think their child is always right regardless of the facts, are always complaining about bullying and spend a lot of time orchestrating their child's friendships. Half-arsed parents run a mile from such crazies. It's no wonder teachers often say it's not kids that drive them to early retirement but parents.

Here are some painful parent types for half-arsed parents and teachers to avoid. It all starts with that one dreaded phrase: *Hi, can I have a quick word?*

The gifted child

Hi, can I have a quick word about my son Aristotle? You know, the gifted one. I'd like to know why he got an F in his essay. I know he only got five words on the page, but I am sure you understand he's too smart to be bound by the conventions of grammar or spelling, word counts or homework tasks. Sometimes I wonder if primary schools are set up to cater for the most talented kids. So, what are your training and qualifications? It must be hard to teach kids like Ari, who is gifted in ways adults like you couldn't possibly understand.

The creative genius

Hi, can I have a quick word about my daughter Gypsy? The principal told me we'd have to pay to have the giant mural she spray-painted on the floor of the classroom removed by professionals. We'd hate to see the erasure of her unique artistic endeavour and had hoped it could be left to be a permanent monument to her free spirit. Yes, I know it looks alarmingly like a giant male appendage bounding across a sky of pubic hair, but can't you see that's evidence of her creative soul flowering?

The bully

Hi, can I have a quick word about my son Brutus? I know it appears he has been punching other kids, but I honestly can't believe it. I asked him straight up if he did it and he said no. I know he doesn't lie to me. He couldn't possibly be at fault. I want to know what the kids he's alleged to have hurt did to provoke him? I've never seen him lift a finger to hurt anyone. Oh sure, there was that time he tied our cat to the exhaust pipe of our car before we drove to Sydney, but he told me it was a science experiment. So clever! Look, the other kid's almost out of hospital, so it can't have been that bad.

The busy bee

Hi, can I have a quick word about your parents' help roster? I'd love to sign up for classroom reading and the zoo excursion, but I don't think you understand how busy I am. There's the kids to look after, and my husband and my friends. Do you know how long it takes to get a spray tan these days, not to mention blonde highlights – four hours, if you're lucky! And, as I am sure you know, Facebook is practically a full-time job in itself! So I'd love to help you, but I am absolutely flat chat. Wait up! Girls! Order me a latte, I'll be there in a minute.

The germ carrier

Hi, can I have a word about my daughter Sally? Look, she has a cold, and a temperature, but she told me she really wants to be at school today. She would be so sad if she had to miss a day. Well, actually, she was begging to stay home but I'm so busy at work I can't afford to be sick. So, I told her she had to soldier on and bring her germs to school rather than spread them around at home. Get her to cough into her elbow. If she needs to lie down, send her to the sick bay – no point ringing me to pick her up as I couldn't possibly leave work early.

The professional volunteer

Hi, can I have a quick word about the way the tuckshop is being run? I was astonished to think these ladies don't have any KPIs to follow, let alone MRKs and PRCs. And how do they know when they've reached the benchmark status required in sausage rolls sales if there isn't an Excel spreadsheet quantifying their progress? Where is the aspiration statement to motivate those staffing the pie-warmer? They're valued team members too. The sandwich-makers aren't as client-focused as they need to be and it's time to think outside the circle and push the envelope and touch base so we can regroup and synergise on the subject of idealised lunchtime toppings. Go Team!

The notice ignorer

Hi, can I have a quick word about the excursion? I know my son brought a notice home from school about it, but he lost it. I can't read all those notices you send anyway. I wonder how you find the time to write them all when we can't find the time to read them! Funny, isn't it? We put a bin in the kitchen because they were cluttering up the bench. So, I thought I'd ask you to tell me what day, what time, what he needs to bring and what the weather will be? Oh sorry, that's my phone, just a minute. It's important. Can you hang on while I take it?

Half-arsed parents don't do or say any of these things. They know it's better to back off and leave the teachers alone. Half-arsed parents respect teachers – most of whom who are passionate, patient and devoted to learning. They rely on teachers to be across their kids' learning, because they are not. And that's okay. Half-arsed parents are glad there's a RateMyTeacher website but no one yet has thought of RateTheParent. They know teachers don't get paid as much as they should and spend most of the summer holidays preparing for the upcoming classes. And half-arsed parents know not to pick a fight with any teacher their younger child is likely to get the following year. Although they'll occasionally bring in a forgotten musical instrument or lunchbox, they butt out and let the kids get on with it. Half-arsed parents let kids succeed – and fail – on their own merits. They will protect their kids from bullies, nits and mullet hairstyles, but they will not protect them from their own lack of effort or achievement.

Chapter 11

TEENAGERS: EAT, DRINK, SLEEP, REPEAT

Aaah, teenagers. They're a special breed of human who think putting on deodorant is the same as having a shower. They don't need a wardrobe because they've got a floor, and when challenged they'll point out that the clean clothes are the ones near the door that haven't been stepped on (yet). They're listening to everything that's being said although they appear to be wearing AirPods and playing with their phone the whole time we speak to them. Their hearing is highly selective. Mine don't appear to hear me asking them to take out the recycling when they're standing next to me, but they can hear me ask them if they want to go and get burgers with their friends when I whisper from another room. Freaky!

Teenagers are also keen to ensure trifles like pressing work commitments don't get in the way of their parents meeting their needs with very little notice. They want their parents to know work deadlines shouldn't stop them from being on time to meet their mates to go see *The Fast and The Furious* for the fifth time in two weeks. They are secure in the knowledge that their social life is much better than ours. These days, I'm lucky to grab a half-drunk glass of wine at my kids' friends' houses in between pick-ups. That's when my teenagers are kind enough to allow me to come to the front door. 'Mum you don't need to get out of the car when you drop me off', they say. 'Give me a twenty and back away from the doorbell.'

Half-arsed parents are realistic about what their teenagers are doing and not doing. They know teens will do their best to demonstrate to their parents that flushing toilets, replacing toilet rolls and putting their plates in the dishwasher are entirely optional choices. They know that their teens like to conduct repeated scientific experiments to show if they wait long enough to do chores, someone else will do it. And yes, in our house, that someone is usually me. Half-arsed parents also know teenagers are self-centred. Their need for expensive brand-name fashion items and lifts on-demand usurp any needs their parents may have, like eating dinner or having enough money for the gas bill. They're also master manipulators. You tell your teenager she must vacuum the car before she can get $10 to buy lunch. By the time the guilt-laden protracted negotiations have finished, you're giving her $20 and cleaning the car yourself.

Half-arsed parents also don't take notice of the poor musical tastes of their teenagers, whose favourite songs have names like 'Hollywood Whores' and lyrics like 'ring, ring, pussy, it's shut down'.

Nor do they indulge teenage girls who wish they grew up in a ghetto so their (non-existent) rap career could have some cred.

Okay, so I am having fun at the expense of the teens in my life. But they don't read books anymore, so I am pretty sure they won't read this one. The reality of most teens' lives is a little less humorous. This is a pretty hard time to be coming of age, and lots of studies report record rates of body image issues, anxiety, depression and social disconnection. I am not trying to solve all serious issues here, but to offer you some tools to help you negotiate the rocky terrain of Planet Teen.

One survey from the Australian Institute of Family Studies of 3000 teens aged 14 and 15 found girls are locked into a battle with their bodies, with many saying they have lost control of their eating. Boys are not immune from such pressures either. One in five males express similar sentiments. In a national mental health snapshot, 8 per cent of girls and 3 per cent of boys reported having suicidal ideations, 6 per cent of girls and 2 per cent of boys made suicidal plans, and 3 per cent of girls and 1 per cent of boys attempted suicide. Few receive medical treatment and most keep their actions secret. These rates are much higher for LGBTQI+ teens. Half-arsed parents aren't half-arsed about the things that matter, such as the mental health of their teenagers. They seek help from friends, family and medical professionals where needed, and not only talk with their teens, but listen to them, too. Social media makes things harder in some ways, and easier in others. It connects teens but also gives them endless opportunities to compete and compare, bitch and bully when they'd be better off doing homework, reading a book, going to sleep or unpacking the dishwasher (no, I won't let that one go).

Unlike hyper-parents, half-arsed parents don't want to be their kids' best friends, drive them to school and manipulate their friendships. Hyper-parents come unravelled when their kids get older and no longer like them, listen to them or care what they say or do. Half-arsed parents don't profess to have all the answers on raising great teenagers. They turn to books written by people like Michael Carr-Gregg and Elly Robinson, Madonna King, Justin Coulson and Andrew Fuller.

Another expert on teens – mainly because she's got two herself – is *Scary Mommy* writer Nancy Friedman. She says get used to the eye rolls and snorts from know-it-all teenagers – they'll come around by the time they're 25. She points out that they hate/ love you, often at the same time. But that's okay because you love/hate them back. Teenagers also have a knack of being 'nice to everyone who isn't you'. As she sees it, this means they're 'confident enough in your love, to let it all hang out when no one else is around'.

Friedman says there will also be some really stupid choices made by the teens in your life. Most of the time nothing bad will happen and they will still be around to tell their own kids about it. Don't forget that their bad choices are just like the bad choices you probably made. I remember going home with a guy I hardly knew because I'd spent my taxi money, walking home late at night by myself after a fight with friends, and not believing my mum when she told me I was gorgeous and strong and amazing.

As Friedman points out, when you are raising teenagers, there will be mess, there will never be enough food and there will be arguments, but you'll get through it all.

I'd love my teens to be more polite, helpful and, once in a while, ask me rather than tell me they need to be driven somewhere. In my mind, the only thing that really matters is that they don't drink and drive. My kids know I'll pay for an Uber or drive across town to pick them up from anywhere, anytime so they never have to drink and drive or get into a car driven by someone who's drunk. I've told them often enough about the time I drove a carful of friends home from a party when I was a teenager. I was so drunk I drove with one eye closed so I didn't see double. It was dark and late and I had to drive through the windy Adelaide Hills. We all made it – God knows how. That one bad mistake could have changed lives forever. I also want my teenagers to use their manners, remember their grandparents' birthdays and – oh yeah – say no to crystal meth.

Here are some more pointers for half-arsed parents who want to keep the upper hand with the smelly, hairy people who have suddenly taken up residence in their house.

Drinking. Yes, they're doing it.

I know all the experts say teenagers shouldn't drink until their brains stop developing or they become mature. This might happen at age 18 or 48. I find it reassuring to let my older son have a beer or two here and there under supervision. I am sure it won't stop him having a technicolour yawn in the roses at some point, but he will be less likely to hide what he's doing from me. The problem with the abstinence approach is that it doesn't work. Most kids will still drink regardless, and they won't ask for help if they drink behind their parents' back because they're worried about getting in trouble. Those whose job it is to monitor teenage parties will tell you kids bring alcohol to parties by 13, and by 14 are experimenting with drugs and sexual behaviour. Half-arsed parents don't presume otherwise.

Findings from the 2020 Australian Secondary Students' Alcohol and Drug Survey show almost half of kids aged 12 to 17 had tried alcohol in the past year and 27 per cent in the last month. Only one-third had never consumed alcohol. Half-arsed parents talk to their kids early about alcohol, drugs and sex, so when they encounter these things themselves, they know what to expect and can make good decisions. This is the advice from two of the wisest teen experts I know, Sacha Kaluri and Sonya Karras, authors of *The Two Worlds of Your Teenager*. They also suggest parents get to know each other, swap mobile numbers and book pre-paid cabs to get kids home safely.

Half-arsed parents are mindful of the fact that the bad choices kids make peak at 16. This is why they will not give their kids a 16th birthday party. Half-arsed parents aren't stupid. They will put off big parties until their child's 21st, when everyone will hopefully be legal and responsible for their own ~~mistakes~~ actions.

Sex. Yes, they're having it.

Oh boy, the world has changed a lot since my sexual education in the 80s, which consisted of a lesson or two about our 'changing bodies' and a practical where we had to roll a condom on a banana. Boys no longer learn about sex from pilfered copies of *Penthouse* or their parents' dog-eared edition of *The Joy of Sex: A Gourmet Guide to Lovemaking*. I remember sneaking into my parents' room to read their copy of this book, written by a guy called Alex Comfort, which I always thought was a very saucy name.

These days, teens are much more likely to be watching hardcore porn on their phones down the back of the school bus or hidden away in their bedrooms. Sadly, this means boys – and, to a lesser extent, girls – are learning that rough, brutal sex is not only normal, but expected. And it's being accessed by kids as young as 11, 88 per cent of whom are watching clips filled with violent images.

Pornography teaches girls to be submissive and grateful, and boys to be domineering and aggressive. A documentary by David Corlett and sex educator Maree Crabbe called *Love and Sex in an Age of Pornography* quotes one young woman saying porn makes it harder to say no to things she is not comfortable with. 'You just have to act like it's amazing.' Both sexes see such material as educational rather than merely recreational. They're using porn as a sexual primer to teach them what to expect from their sexual encounters. As Crabbe puts it, children are 'initiating the signature sex acts from pornography'. In many cases, they're discovering pornography before they encounter sex, which changes what they think is normal.

Half-arsed parents don't really want to talk about any of this, especially with their teenagers. But they know they have to talk to their sons and daughters about the sexualised material out there. They are not in denial; they assume any child from about age 11 onwards has access to pornography and could be watching it. Half-arsed parents teach their daughters sex should be pleasurable and mutual, and never violent or scary. They teach boys sex should not be about them being dominant over a submissive female. Sex for boys, too, should be pleasurable and mutual. They teach them all about the dangers of sharing inappropriate images and engaging in online sexual harassment. And perhaps they find an old copy of *The Joy of Sex* for them to read and marvel at all the free-range pubic hair.

Don't muck up muck-up day

Half-arsed parents love the idea of year 12 finally coming to an end – for them as much as for the kids. They love the idea of muck-up days and think it's a disgrace it's been mucked up by uptight nanny-staters trying to turn it into a fun-free Celebration Day. Half-arsed parents don't believe the rites of passage that have been meaningful for generations of Australians should be sanitised or erased because those in power are going through a mid-life crisis. The fun police partied their way through the 70s and 80s, and now they're in positions of influence, they're doing everything they can to ensure anything enjoyable is seen as life-threatening or illegal.

Sadly, schools are cracking down on muck-up days by banning flour bombs, eggings and dress-up marches in favour of barbecues, sporting matches and formal events. What a total yawn-fest. One teacher even boasted that his school replaced muck-up day with a 'dinner with parents' and a 'few games on the oval'. That's not fun, that's funereal. Of course there needs to be some ground rules for muck-up day. Don't harm animals. Don't get arrested. Avoid the hospital emergency department. Ideally, neither the police nor the fire brigade will be needed. But a ban on water pistols when it's 30 degrees? That's ridiculous.

Half-arsed parents remember what it was like to be a teenager. They know muck-up day is not a celebration but a day of reckoning, revenge and revolt. After 13 years of being told what to do, it's the one day when kids can get even with teachers. It's meant to be subversive, wild and a little crazy.

From year nine onwards, muck-up day was just about all we talked about (apart from the spunks at the boys' school down the road). Would we kidnap the headmistress with water pistols and demand a ransom? What about releasing three mice numbered 1, 2 and 4 into a classroom and watching the teacher freak out trying to find number 3? Or should we put a 'For Sale' sign outside the school block or take photos of all the teachers' cars and post them for sale in the *Trading Post*? In the end, we wore homemade fluoro tutus (it was the 80s, after all), and attacked the school with rolls of toilet paper and water pistols. We ripped up our dresses, flour-bombed each other and wrote dodgy things about teachers on the concrete paths with shaving cream. We broke into the boys' school and scattered around tampons because the week before they'd drawn the outline of a penis in weed killer on our oval. Good times.

Now, some schools don't even allow kids to sign their dresses and shirts while they are wearing them for fear of sexual harassment complaints. Half-arsed parents don't approve of such over-protectiveness. But they do have one rule. They don't let their kids go too hard at muck-up day because they know there's still schoolies to come.

Schoolies – go hard, then go home

I finished school in 1987 and a group of us headed down to an SA coastal town for a week. Photos from the time show a very tame group of girls with bad skin, baggy jeans and mousy bobs (maybe it was just me) trying to catch the eye of sexually repressed boys who looked like members of Duran Duran in very low light. Throwing up in a stranger's rubbish bin or getting chucked out of the Hotel Victor for being under-age was about as crazy as it got. Back then, it was accepted that parents were around to drive us and help clean up the mess. We didn't care they were there – we were grateful to be finished year 12 and hanging out with our friends at the beach.

Things have changed. Now, there's an overwhelming sense of entitlement among school-leavers that dictates parents aren't allowed to have anything to do with schoolies, let alone be anywhere near the actual event. But our teenagers still kindly let us pay for it. Local beaches are now seen as too close to home, and anything less than Bali, Thailand or the Gold Coast isn't cool enough. Apparently, the big new schoolies destination is Vanuatu. Of course it is.

At schoolies, the T-shirts tell the real story. Girls wear tops saying, 'Don't bother, I'm not drunk yet'. Boys' shirts sport slogans such as, 'Good Evening Bitches' and 'Plastered'. Others shirts read, 'Check in, sneak in grog, hit the beach, beer o'clock, scope talent, hook up, grab kebab, repeat'. I was at Surfers Paradise one year during schoolies (big mistake). I noticed a shop called Condom Kingdom selling a Schoolies Showbag. $20 bought you a bonking calendar, love dice, condoms and a pack of cards with 52 insults. Nice.

Social media has also upped the ante, offering new platforms for kids to get attention by doing dangerous and crazy things. If you've ever wondered what kids really get up to at schoolies, head to Facebook and Instagram sites such as 'Schoolies Gone Wild' and 'Schoolies Fails'. You will see kids pouring cask wine directly into each other's mouths and passed out drunk surrounded by empty bottles. Others are smoking drugs or drinking from beer bongs. Despite the official alcohol-free, drug-free mantra, the reality is obviously very different.

Half-arsed parents are aware of what can go wrong, but they also know the vast majority of kids do nothing more than party hard then go home. Most young people of 17 or 18 know how to look after their mates and know the difference between getting drunk and getting totally wasted. Many have some sexual experience, and have been drinking for some time. Thanks to ID badges, wristbands, free meals, free buses and volunteer helpers, schoolies is safer than it first appears.

Half-arsed parents will let their kids go to schoolies, but they'll set the ground rules and expect them to be adhered to. For me, it's no high-rises, no overseas locations and they must always pick up when I ring to check how they are. They must stay with their friends and always look out for each other. Half-arsed parents won't let teenagers dictate terms. They'll do what they need to do to make sure their kids come home safely (and use the condoms as well as the bonking calendar).

Teen talk: a guide for half-arsed parents

Raising teenagers is tricky. Teens don't really like being told what to do – that's when they bother to listen in the first place. But it's time to relax or, as they'd say, *chillax*. Half-arsed parents know knowledge is power. Understanding what's going on in teenage heads will give parents an edge. Here's a guide to decoding what's really going on with the surly strangers your sweet kids have become. You won't be surprised to know there's a big gap between what teenagers say and what they mean.

They say: *I'll be there in a minute.*
They mean: I'll be there in many minutes – as many as
  I need. In fact, I am going to ignore you so many times
  you will forget the trivial household chore you were going
  to ask me to do.

They say: *There's nothing to eat.*

They mean: By telling you the fridge is empty, I am trying to make you feel unworthy as a parent and more likely to pay for pizza.

They say: *I don't have any homework.*

They mean: Well, I do have maths homework but I don't understand it and I am not a nerd like you who thinks homework is necessary. You'd have to pull the wi-fi out of the house for me to do it tonight because a new season of *13 Reasons Why* has hit Netflix and I need to work out why Hannah did it. Maths isn't on my radar. Wait. What's a radar?

They say: *I'm tired.*

They mean: I know you asked me to unpack the dishwasher but I know that if I pretend to be tired for long enough you'll get sick of the dirty dishes on the sink and do it yourself.

They say: *Can I have some money to top up my train card?*

They mean: I can't ask for money for lunch because you'll either give me four dollars in 20c pieces or make me a salad sandwich. So I ask for train money. We both know I don't ever use my train card, but it's a lie we both seem willing to accept.

Parent says: *Dinner's ready.*

Teen says: *Just one more game.*

Teen means: We both know games like this never end.
If you let me, I'll say 'one more game' for the next
48 hours.

Teen says: *Should I sweep the front driveway?*

Teen means: I've ordered a Halal Snack Pack with extra
mayo on your UberEats account and need to be out the
front when it's delivered.

Parent says: *Have you had a shower lately?*

Teen says: *(sniffs armpits and makes a face) Nah, I'm good.*

Teen means: My armpit smells like something died up
there but I can put up with it if you can.

Half-arsed parents know there's a certain look that teenagers use when they're forced to stop what they're doing (even though it's almost certainly nothing) and give us some face time. It's a mixture of boredom, pity, amusement and hunger. Remember, they're not conversing with us, they're biding time until they can get back on their phone/laptop/video game. But half-arsed parents don't stress. They don't overparent and they don't intervene unless it's needed. And they do not micro-manage their teenagers' lives and then act surprised when they can't make choices for themselves.

Good luck with your adventures raising teens. Trust me, you'll need it.

Chapter 12

TECHNOLOGY: TAMING THE DIGITAL NATIVES

It's hard for today's digital natives to understand the tech-free world we grew up in. Back then, our fathers and mothers were our Google, our local libraries were our internet and radio stations were our Spotify. Kids today don't know how to look things up manually in phonebooks, library card catalogues, dictionaries or maps. They will never get to book flights seven, 14 or 21 days ahead, get film developed at a chemist or go backpacking with Lonely Planet guidebooks weighing them down. We feel sorry for young people who miss out on all of these things. In turn, they judge us for texting with one finger rather than both thumbs.

When I was growing up, there was only one TV with four channels: 2, 7, 9 and 10. This meant we watched what was on – whether it was *Play School*, *The Goodies* or *Pot Black*. It's a concept that's foreign to kids today, accustomed to TV-on-demand and 24-hour movies and shows on their own individual screens. It makes parents yearn for the togetherness that comes from watching a TV show as a family. You know, back when you all watched one screen in one room, guaranteeing that whatever was on, no one really wanted to watch.

Times have changed and we're now all teched-up. You can buy belts that automatically loosen when you've had too much to eat, $200 socks 'infused with proprietary 100% textile sensors' and wine bottles that connect to the internet. Even basic appliances like fridges are smarter than the people using them. They're not only about keeping food cold, but 'food management', 'entertainment options' and 'connectivity'. I say no. I don't want my fridge to create a 'unique profile' for me that tells my whole family I stayed up last night eating cookie dough ice cream.

The challenge for half-arsed parents is to give kids the best bits of our childhoods supplemented – rather than dominated – by the tech advances of today. Screens are a vital sanity saver for parents and doing without them, or severely limiting kids' time on them, is not going to happen. It reminds me of that meme that says, 'Sure, I could parent without screen time. I could churn my own butter but let's not get crazy here.' I still feel ripped-off that I had to raise my first son without the benefit of tablets or smartphones. All I had to keep me from going crazy was a collection of badly scratched Wiggles DVDs. (I watched them so often I once had a special adult dream about Greg, the original yellow Wiggle.)

Half-arsed parents aren't anti-tech, although we definitely don't want wine bottles that divulge our secrets. We think being connected to phones, tablets and laptops makes us better parents. It makes the boring bits of parenting bearable and enables a bit of multitasking. Thanks to my iPhone, I can text my friends while stirring the risotto for dinner. I can knock off some work emails while waiting for the kids to finish footy. And I can make sure I don't miss that urgent waxing appointment before the parents' race at the kids' swimming carnival. It drives my kids crazy, but I also love texting. I love texting so much I text my friends to ask them if they're free to text. I text my kids in the next room to tell them to stop texting and do their homework. But I had to stop using voice-activated texts at work because of all the mis-heard texts about going to 'pussy ranches' and cooking 'children's fingers' for dinner.

This is why half-arsed parents do not agree with one parenting fad urging them to be 'hands-free' and ditch the phones altogether. The idea of raising kids without using technology makes me see red (thank God for red-eye correction on my iPhone). We know for ourselves when to put down the iPhone and give our kids some face time (and no, I don't mean through the phone). Half-arsed parents will not be guilted into thinking our children must be the one thing we focus on at all times. It would be a nightmare.

Half-arsed parents think kids need to know they're not the centre of the universe. Time pressures and competing demands don't make us bad parents; they make us normal. Yes, we need to make sure there is balance. Perhaps we should put down the iPad when we're listening to our kid doing their nightly reader (or at least turn the sound off). Half-arsed parents know they are doing a good enough job with their hands full. There's no need for us to put down our phones and be hands-free.

Younger kids are not at risk

Two-thirds of young children are spending more time on screens than national guidelines recommend. You may think this is cause for concern, but it's because the guidelines are ridiculous. Let's not blame the parents, but federal bodies that are out of touch with modern ways of raising kids. For instance, the Australian guidelines say children under two should not look at screens at all, and kids aged two to five should not be in front of screens for more than one hour a day. Kids aged five to 17 can have two hours a day. A Queensland study of 3000 parents shows kids under two spend 50 minutes in front of screens on weekdays and 58 minutes on weekends. And kids aged two to five watch 90 minutes a day on average. Screen time plateaus at 94 minutes a day around the age of three, and then reduces once kids start school or go to childcare. If my kids are anything to go by, it increases once they hit late primary school and then again when they become teenagers.

These figures hardly add up to a national catastrophe for younger kids. Screens keep them occupied, which allows parents to do the things they need to do. The concern is that kids are missing out on other activities and playtime when they're on screens, but 50 to 90 minutes of screen time a day leaves many, many hours for active play. It's time for a sensible debate that starts with screen time as a given. Rather than act as if screens are toxic, it would be more useful to give parents tips on managing and setting limits rather than ruling them out altogether. Doctors in the United Kingdom don't set such restrictions. A panel of UK researchers say there's little evidence that reasonable screen time is having a detrimental impact.

Admittedly, some kids are screen addicts. I have seen children who scream when the phone is taken away or throw a tantrum if they have to hand over the iPad. There's no doubt some parents take it too far. Kids don't need to be glued to an iPhone while they're being wheeled around the supermarket for ten minutes. Kids don't need to be handed a screen to help them get through a five-minute car ride. Kids don't need to be on a screen while they're in a pram on a walk. Automatically handing a kid a screen with *The Lion King* or *Frozen* on high rotation every time there's a quiet moment means they don't ever learn to entertain themselves or get bored.

However, most parents don't do this, so it's insulting for so-called experts to count the minutes our younger kids spend in front of screens. Further, studies show mothers whose kids spend a lot of time on screens are likely to be experiencing financial and emotional stress. Let's give these parents more support to curb excessive screen time rather than demonise them and everyone else.

Screenagers

Managing screens is harder as children get older. My two older kids – who are both teens – are surgically attached to their phones, and use Apple's virtual assistant Siri 300 or so times a day. Mostly it's voice-dictating messages asking me to bring them food while they're lying in bed. Manually typing or texting is so last century. Thanks to Siri, students could take three seconds flat to find out the average rainfall in the Peruvian basin, the molarity of hypochlorite or the plot of *Romeo and Juliet*. But they don't. They're looking up things they should know anyway. 'Hey Siri, what's seven times two?', 'Hey Siri, what's an adjective?', 'Hey Siri, how can I earn money from my bedroom after school without my parents finding out?'.

By the time they're teenagers, 70 per cent of kids spend too much time on tablets, phones, video games and computers, according to a survey of 2600 Australian mums and dads by the Parenting Research Centre. This is much more of an issue for the parents of teenagers than younger kids. Luckily, there is a whole heap of great advice on this issue. Half-arsed parents don't have to go through this alone. They might take advice from someone like Dr Kristy Goodwin, who's written *Raising Your Child in a Digital World*. She says parents should formulate a family media plan to help kids form good screen habits. She suggests starting with 24 hours, then subtracting the time needed for sleep (including naps), school, kindergarten or childcare, play, activities and family time, movement and eating. The time left over may be allotted to screens without it leading to developmental or health problems.

Another pathway is offered by Brad Marshall, an Australian psychologist who's helped hundreds of families address gaming disorder. His book *The Tech Diet for your Child and Teen* says controlling the wi-fi is the key to helping curb the addiction of kids to screen and computer games. 'I'm not suggesting you should pack your kids in the car and go off-grid like there's a zombie apocalypse upon us,' Marshall told me recently. Rather, he suggests parents take control of the internet connection in their homes. 'Your best course of action is to find a mobile phone plan that gives your child very limited data, so you can control the wi-fi. Put simply, you need the ability to turn the internet off. This will allow you to reframe the internet as a reward, not a right. Then it becomes every parent's most powerful bargaining chip.' I like his approach. His excellent little book suggests giving teenagers a mobile plan providing between 1GB and 5GB per month, which makes them reliant on the home wi-fi most of the time.

Marshall also advocates using apps that allow parents to create individual profiles for each member of the family. 'Use it to disable all features apart from the basic ones like phone calls, alarms and music between certain hours. If your child goes to bed at 9 pm, you could set up their phone to become incredibly boring between 8.30 pm and 7 am.' Marshall doesn't advocate taking away part of the game consoles, like the controller, warning that kids often end up buying their own and hiding them in their rooms.

Marshall and others stress that parents need to be aware of the signs of screen addiction. Half-arsed parents take this seriously. They love it when technology means they have a bit more 'me time' on the couch, but they worry when they haven't seen their teen for 72 hours. Warning signs include changes in behaviour, kids who don't sleep, secret crying, unexplained high emotions, a drop in grades, missing school, swearing and verbal aggression at home, declining invitations from friends to go out and secretly staying up late or getting up early to fit in more screen time.

Another excellent source is mother-of-five Martine Oglethorpe, who is a trusted eSafety provider with the Office of the eSafety Commissioner. Her book *The Modern Parent* says parents need to move beyond taking the phones off their kids as a punishment and teach them to use technology safely and confidently. This includes helping kids to assess critically what they encounter on screens and work out what's real and what's fake.

My friends manage phones and screens in different ways. Some insist on knowing their kids' passwords and having 24/7 access to their social media accounts and apps. This makes sense, as long as they know the more hands-on they are, the more likely kids are to have another phone or account which they keep hidden. A few years ago, one of the footy mums found her son left his second Insta account open on her phone. All the mums got excited, passing her phone around and checking out the secret accounts of our kids. Most were pretty much the same as their first accounts, but with more swearing.

Other parents insist on no social media until the kids are 13 or even older. The only problem with this is that they're probably going to be on Snapchat or Instagram a year or two earlier than this. If they're going behind their parents' backs, they may not speak up if they encounter a serious cyberbullying or harassment issue. Others use apps such as Family Time to control their kids' social media time – giving them an hour after homework has been completed or an hour before bed. If kids muck up, their phone is disabled. This tends to work best with younger kids and is hard to enforce when kids use their phones for homework. Others say they don't mind too much what the kids do, as long as their phone is plugged in and charging in the kitchen by 9 pm.

Video games aren't the devil's work

Video games are another battleground for parents. I know this firsthand, as my younger son loves computer games. Once, he came into the living room and told me he'd had three kills. 'It was GREAT, Mum', he said. He'd been playing Fortnite, a game where 100 players parachute onto an island, each initially armed with only a pickaxe. Then they fight each other with a collection of cross-bows, rifles, snipers and grenade launchers. The last fighter standing is the winner. It's got 40 million players, so your kids are probably playing it with their friends, even if you don't know about it.

Australian data from a survey of more than 6000 kids shows 85 per cent of kids aged 11 to 17 play electronic games. One quarter play less than one hour on weekends, and less than ten per cent play nine hours or more. Only 3.9 per cent exhibit problem behaviours. We need to focus our efforts on curbing these excessive users rather than demonising all kids for playing computer games without harm. Half-arsed parents don't buy into the hysteria some people have against video games. They know violent games have been around for years, and they probably played them as kids.

Experts have different ideas about how to manage kids' video use. Some say it's a good idea for parents to play video games with their kids. No thanks. I love the time off these games give me. Others suggest parents should tune into their kids' headphones so they know what they are doing in the game. Again, this is not something I'd ever do. Helicopter parenting has never been my style – especially when it's Black Hawk Special Ops. Give me *Bachelor in Paradise* and *Grand Designs* reruns instead. Half-arsed parents know Fortnite and games like it are the ultimate parental bribe material. 'Hey kids, wanna parachute to the island? Just clean your room, do your homework and make dinner while I try and work out what's going on with Jarrod and Keira in Fiji.'

My kids' obsession with Fortnite made me realise how much computer games have changed since I was a kid. I used to play Leisure Suit Larry in the Land of the Lounge Lizards with my dad. I remember helping Larry – a boxy, pixelated 38-year-old virgin who lived in his mother's basement – get laid. In a series of seedy adventures, Larry would pick up prostitutes, get drunk in bars, dance the night away at a disco, fraternise with women in penthouse hot tubs and lose money at the casino. All of this didn't turn me into a raging, liquored-up loser Lothario with empty pockets, did it? No. Well, not really.

This is why half-arsed parents don't assume Fortnite and other games are going to turn our kids into mini GI Joes. If kids start bringing axes to school, then they've got more problems than could be caused by a mere game. Half-arsed parents don't stress about video games unless their kids are fully hooked. Then, they take drastic action. They control their use by limiting the wi-fi, turning off the consoles and forcing kids outside. Kids who make a fuss are punished with longer tech-free times. Half-arsed parents know video games are part of growing up and fitting in with others. At this point, Fortnite is so hot it's already starting to fade, my world-weary teen said the other day.

'What's the next big thing?' I asked him.

'Footy,' he said.

Aaaah. As much as some things change, they also stay the same.

Do what works for you – not just the kids

Half-arsed parents aren't afraid to say no when they think kids have had enough screens, and there are consequences if the kids are sneaky or make a fuss. When no doesn't work, we remove phones, tablets, laptops or game consoles. Or we change the wi-fi password and let the kids come begging. Sometimes it suits us to give them phones, such as if they're going on a bike ride. Being able to contact them lets us give them more freedom. (The anti-phone brigade forgets this important point.)

Kids shouldn't make all the decisions. Whatever rules you set have to work for all of you, not just them. Half-arsed parents accept screens are part of our lives, but kids need to learn when to put them down. For instance, when we're talking to them, when they're in class and when they are crossing the road. And we need to get them used to managing screens according to their own judgments as they get older, not merely following instructions from us.

I personally don't need to see every text or post from my kids, and I don't use time controls or apps. I'm a bit more hands-off. In my house, kids who do well at school get a lot more flexibility with their phones. When the grades drop, phone time gets slashed. I am also not afraid to take the phone away altogether, sometimes for a week, as a punishment. My kids only get basic phones from year five onwards so they can be contactable, and then smartphones with social media when they hit high school. This gives them time to enjoy a bit of screen-free life like we did. One of my rules is no screens at the dinner table. I'm getting very good at spotting the teenagers with their phones on their laps pretending to look pensive because of the serious cutting-edge political dinnertime conversation. In fact, they're sending streaks on Snapchat and trying not to get caught. (Sending streaks is different to streaking, in case you're wondering.)

I'd prefer to spend my time educating my kids about cyber-bullying, not micro-managing their screen time. I try to make the most of 'teachable moments' – in other words, f*ck-ups. One such moment was finding out a friend's son had posted a caption about 'gay nigs' on Instagram. Another friend's daughter was blackmailed by a guy she liked. He asked her to send him some topless shots and when she said she didn't want to, he said he'd tell everyone she was a 'frigid bitch'. Another was finding out a friend's daughter had started a 'Hot or Not' list of their friends. Kids have always been nasty at times, but the online setting provides a ripple effect that spreads the impact of bullying like never before. Half-arsed parents know that talking through such issues will help our kids develop a sound radar and make good judgments.

Half-arsed parents teach kids that nothing can be fully deleted from social media. They must be accountable for everything. They should apply the front page of the newspaper test. How would they feel if the text or message they thought was private ended up on the front page of the paper? (Or the home screen of BuzzFeed?) They need to think about others when they post or message in a group. And they need to know that if they are part of a group sharing unauthorised photos of minors then they are as culpable as anyone else, even if they didn't post the shots. That's right; the boy who demands, receives or disseminates nude photos of a girl can end up on a sex offenders registry. In most cases, a little education can prevent life-long labels of criminality.

Managing our kids' use of technology is one of the biggest issues facing parents today. Half-arsed parents reject the techno-guilt and catastrophising around phones, video games and screens. They accept kids are digital natives and put in strategies governing screen use rather than obsess about the kids being on them in the first place.

Chapter 13

CELEBRATIONS: UNDERWHELM AND UNDERPERFORM

Parents need to apply the key half-arsed messages to special days as well as every day. Birthdays, Christmas, Mother's Day and Father's Day are all times when many parents (mostly mums) indulge in a big serve of one-upmanship with a side order of humblebragging. Half-arsed parents often can't be bothered impressing anyone, and will underwhelm, under-perform and cut corners on these occasions wherever possible. Half-arsed parents don't have the time, money or motivation to turn every family milestone into a massive Insta-worthy show complete with colour-coded dessert bar, themed gifts, dress-ups and extravagant entertainment. These days, you don't have a party, you have an 'event'. You don't have food, you have 'catering'. And kids don't play games, they have 'entertainment'. Yep, we've put the 'sell' in celebration.

Birthday parties – just buy the cake, will you?

When we were young, birthday parties involved mum pulling out her dog-eared copy of the *Women's Weekly* cake book and asking her kids to pick which one they wanted. If your mother didn't manage to produce the train cake, or the pool cake with jelly on top or the farmyard one with chocolate malt sticks around the edge, you knew she didn't love you enough. It was a lot of pressure. One friend told me she found out years later her mother glued some of the book's pages together so her kids wouldn't choose the hard ones. And yet the cakes were pretty basic in today's terms. They were often packet cake mixes with butter cream and lots of lollies to hide the wonky bits.

My, how things have changed. Back then, parties were in backyards with games run by mums and dads and the food was fairy bread, party pies and watermelon wedges. That was in the days before musical chairs had to have the same number of chairs to children so no one got out. In the past decade, every party my kids have been to – or thrown themselves – has involved either going somewhere (trampolining, movies, the zoo) or bringing in entertainment (clowns, superheroes, fairies, jumping castles). In one generation, we've managed to turn something that should be fun and easy into yet another chore we end up outsourcing at great expense. Half-arsed parents know every over-the-top party our kids go to further entrenches their sense of entitlement and expectation. Half-arsed parents are all for outsourcing, but such showstopping events often end up being much more work and much more expensive than they need to be.

I've watched kids at the rare, casual backyard parties they occasionally get invited to. You can see them looking around somewhat nervously: is this all? Where's the jumping castle? Where's Batman? Where is the lady dressed as a woodland fairy handing out ladybird cupcakes? Half an hour later, most are on a red-cordial high and blissfully enjoying something they don't often get these days: unstructured free time to play.

Half-arsed parents draw inspiration from the parties of their youth. They do the passable minimum, picking one thing to do well and skimping or slacking on the rest. For me, that's usually meant paying for an entertainer to come to our house for a couple of hundred dollars but doing the food myself and skipping decorations entirely. My birthday cake stand-by is an ice-cream cake made from two litres of cheapie vanilla melted into a cake tin and topped with a tower of pre-frozen ice-cream balls in different colours. I ripped off the idea from a well-known ice-cream shop because I once refused to pay $85 for a kid's birthday cake. It's different and that's what makes it a hit. You can even do it drunk. Don't ask me how I know that.

After 16 years of raising kids, I've learnt a few things about birthday parties. I know you can't use cheap snakes in red jelly cups because their colour seeps and they look like dead man's fingers suspended in blood. I know not to make a chocolate cake covered in desiccated coconut like I did one year – it looked like a guy with dandruff had left his wig on the table. And I know rainbow marble cakes feel like a good idea but invariably look as if a kid ate fairy bread then threw up in a baking tin.

I have to admit that I'm not immune to parental party fever. I had a very bad case of affluenza for my elder son's first birthday. The party was totally over the top. There were 50 guests, two buffet tables with homemade sweet and savoury treats, 100 colour-coded balloons, and two dozen bottles of wine with specially customised labels with our son's photo on them. The only thing missing was his name and birth date written in the sky by aeroplane, but only because I didn't think of it in time. Everything was in the party theme colours of cornflower blue and pale yellow, and it had to look perfect. Actually, it had to be better than perfect, it had to look AMAZING. It had to be the best party anyone had EVER been to.

The self-imposed pressure of it all sent me insane. All that effort and expense was for a one-year-old who would have been happy with a wading pool of coloured balls and a plate of watermelon. That, incidentally, is all he got the following year because I learnt my lesson. My son doesn't remember a thing about his first party, but that's probably because it wasn't about him anyway; it was all about me. You'll be pleased to know that after the first birthday extravaganza, I've opted for much more low-key events for the other kids.

Famous people celebrating the inevitable ability of their children to grow older each year have helped fuel this party trend towards excess. The Family Values report suggests seven in ten parents think social media and celebrities put more pressure on them to throw visually impressive parties they can share with others online. A few years ago, Kim Kardashian and Kanye West threw a party for their little baby, North. The event was called 'Kidchella', a play on the Coachella music festival. The extravaganza included a Ferris wheel, moon bounce, dress-ups and a three-tiered rainbow birthday cake. Adults outnumbered kids ten to one, as they do at most first birthday parties. It was a global sensation covered in all the media, but even that wasn't enough, with some people panning Kim K's choice of baby shoes as 'pathetic' and her choice of baby outfit as 'ugly'. Half-arsed parents don't bother competing in the first place; they know they'll never win and they don't really care to try.

Half-arsed parents opt out of the competitive party scene because they know they don't care enough (or spend enough) to throw *the best parties ever*. Over time, they've managed to lower expectations by keeping their own kids happy, but not doing enough to impress anyone else. No one wins in the game of hyper-parenting and half-arsed parents are smart enough not to bother trying.

The Family Values report shows more than two in five parents say they have judged others for having overly extravagant celebrations. But only 13 per cent say they could be accused of being too extravagant themselves with their own children's birthday celebrations. Psychologists call this 'illusory superiority': people think the criticisms they have of others don't apply to them personally. Funnily enough, only seven per cent of parents say they have judged other parents on their child's birthday party or other celebrations for being too modest and simple. Pity. Modesty and simplicity are half-arsed hallmarks.

When it comes to birthday cakes, half-arsed parents ignore all the humblebragging on social media. Chances are they not serving up a nine-turret three-tier *Tangled* birthday cake with fondant icing and candied figurines they've spent 76 hours baking from scratch. They're more likely to doll up a supermarket vanilla cake with two kilos of lollies and watch *Nailed It!* instead of baking into the wee hours. *Nailed It!* shows home bakers trying to recreate fancy cakes made by professionals. Most of the time, they do very badly. Their cakes collapse, only get half made and look nothing like they're meant to, with uneven icing, lurid over-coloured fondant and wonky drunken writing and decorations. Half-arsed parents raise a glass to these half-arsed heroes. We salute you because your new low standards make the rest of us look good.

Christmas Day – overpromise and underdeliver

The idea for this book came from a column I wrote about having a half-arsed Christmas. It was 2016 and my aim was to 'cut corners, diminish expectations and underwhelm my loved ones at every opportunity'. I wrote that 'I just can't be bothered with doing anything much this year; I don't want to not live up to the high expectations I think others have of me.'

I still feel the same way. Half-arsed parents want to take the pressure out of the festive period. Half-arsed parents say yes to Kris Kringles. They say yes to store-bought turkey pieces, pre-prepared salads and plum pudding out of a tin. They say yes to everyone bringing a dish, extensive use of paper plates and uncles doing the washing up. And they say yes to spending more money on alcohol. It won't make the food taste better, but they'll care less about what everyone thinks.

Half-arsed parents are time-poor and cash-strapped and will return to short-cuts that have served them well in the past. They reuse, recycle and regift where they think they can get away with it – hoping they don't get back all the dud gifts they gave their friends last year. They will give family members money for Christmas even though it means they will know how much they're loved in dollar terms (not very much). They will clean the bits of the house on public display and hide clutter in cupboards. Half-arsed parents might remember to turn on the Christmas lights strung in the tree still up from last year. Or they might not.

And yet this doesn't stop me from approaching every Christmas season thinking it's going to be different this time, and I am going to create a showstopping event for once. Every year in early November, I start dreaming about how fabulous this year's festive feast is going to be. I fork out big bucks on the Christmas editions of all the cooking mags, and pore over the beautifully styled spreads containing blonde-haired children in outfits colour-matched to the food. I become seduced by dishes such as profiterole trifle, root vegetable tarte tartin and mushroom and kale croissant pudding in *Taste*, even though I am not even sure what any of them are.

Never has so little culinary success been preceded by so much optimism. In *delicious.* magazine, Matt Preston suggests Damascene raspberry and saffron pavlova, which looks like an edible opera house. My house will end up more drama scene than

Damascene – especially when the kids realise their much-loved pav has been given a trendy make-over with saffron and is now bright yellow.

It's the same when it comes to Christmas crafts. Pinterest wants me to turn my pool noodles into a giant wreath for the side of my house. It wants me to repurpose toilet rolls into Christmas tree decorations (use the toilet paper first, they usefully suggest). And it wants me to paint a Christmas tree using a fork and acrylics on the living room wall. Half-arsed parents say no to all of these ludicrous suggestions. The only thing I'll do with pool noodles is give them to my kids instead of the pool they asked for.

All my fancy plans go out the window because I am a half-arsed parent, not a hyper-parent. In mid-December, I realise I have two weeks to buy 46 presents, decorate the house, put up the tree and prepare and cook three courses for 14 people including two vegans and someone who is fructose intolerant. Making matters worse, I'm working until the 23rd and have to juggle 16 school and work functions and 56 end-of-year sporting events for the kids.

Despite this, there is no end of people offering advice on how half-arsed parents should lift their game and amp-up Christmas. Donna sodding Hay wants to make sure we serve up 'a little bit of magic to create that sense of excitement and wonder that comes with this time of the year'. Well, in my house, things are so low-key that the sense of excitement comes when the kids work out I haven't totally forgotten Christmas. The wonder will come when they realise there actually are presents, even though they are still in the shopping bags, complete with receipts to make the inevitable returns easier.

Christmas presents – regift, reuse and refuse

One Christmas, I gave the son of a dear friend of mine an ugly rubber dog's head that made gross farting and burping noises. It's the kind of toy hungover parents who can't get the lid off the kid-safe aspirin bottle really, really hate. This gift started a competition between my friend and me. In return, she gave my son a Furby. This nasty little technicolour terror doesn't have an off switch and doesn't shut up. Ever. Furby sat on the bookshelf in my son's room and sniggered, snorted, farted and laughed maniacally until it accidentally fell in a big wet bucket of STFU and was never seen again.

Then I returned the favour by giving my friend's son a packet of Hexbug Nanos, tiny little electronic insects that scurry around the room. They promptly fell into her heating ducts and could be heard for weeks, buzzing around under her floor. Cost: $400 in ducted heating cleaning. Revenge: Priceless. (She got me back by signing me and my partner up for a Christian seniors swingers website, but that's another story.)

The hardest part of Christmas is working out what to buy everyone. I don't care about what anyone gets me. I don't want perfume. I want quality time with my family that doesn't involve school functions, office Christmas parties or battling crowds at shopping centres. I don't want soap. I want time to relax by a pool with a trashy novel. And I don't want lingerie. I just want the 25th of December to be over. That's when the real family time begins – not to mention all the Christmas sales where you can return all the things you didn't want and buy things you do want for half the price.

A few men I know do all their Christmas shopping at five o'clock on Christmas Eve and buy only three different presents: booze for the men, perfume for the ladies and chocs for the oldies. Half-arsed parents should adopt this approach.

It's even worse when you are buying for kids. Kids these days are smart. They prepare metre-long Christmas wish-lists of whatever annoying expensive toys are being advertised on TV. Then Grandma helps them to post the list to Santa, and they receive a reply from the North Pole, cementing their expectation that they will get everything they want. On Christmas Day, there's recriminations, protestations and tears as they realise you, their tight-arse, thoughtless parents, bought them a soccer ball and a cricket bat rather than $5000 worth of PS4 games involving bloodshed. Shame on you.

Two of my kids have birthdays in December and late November, so they're over it all by the end of December. 'Just give me money,' says one. 'Vouchers,' says another, not taking her eyes off her iPhone. It's just as hard with younger kids, with over-indulged toddlers having meltdowns because they've run out of gifts to open by 7 am on Christmas Day. By mid-morning, they go fully feral and start opening other people's presents in a frenzy of gift-lust. 'Where's the next one?' they scream, tearing paper from any present within reach.

Half-arsed parents try not to ask their kids what presents they want. It gives them high expectations that will never be met. They keep them away from the toy catalogues so they don't know what they're missing out on, and make sure they know they won't get everything on their list – or anything in fact. It all goes back to the great present fiasco of 1976 when I spent Christmas Day in tears because my parents bought me the wrong type of Derwent pencils. Watercolour! What were they thinking? My grandma saved the day by giving me some new long white socks for me to wear to school with my roman sandals. True story.

The big-ticket item for kids these days are trampolines, which now come for as little as $169. But be warned: the $169 trampoline will cost you dearly. In six months, the netting will have decayed, in 12 months the poles will be falling down, and it will become an unsightly metal death trap beloved by children of all ages. Half-arsed parents will regret the decision to buy one, because they'll spend 12 torturous hours on Christmas Eve putting it together by car headlight, lamenting their decision to drink a six-pack first. And their friends will wonder why they bought the el cheapo one rather than their $984 springfree model that still looks like new five years down the track.

Lego is also a big seller. Sadly, though, these days just about all you can buy are kits producing complicated branded vehicles like the Star Wars Pre Vizsla's Mandalorian Fighter (huh?). Half-arsed dads will spend Christmas afternoon, full of shiraz and misplaced nostalgia, trying to put one of these things together.

It will take three weeks, and by the end of the process father and child will be barely speaking. When it is finally finished, it will live on a high shelf. Something that took Dad so long to put together is too precious to be actually played with.

This year, my present to myself will be to give my kids nothing, film their crazed reactions and watch it go viral on YouTube.

Mother's Day

Half-arsed mums think Mother's Day is like a dose of foot fungus. It always comes back sooner than we'd like. Half-arsed mums would like Mother's Day to be a real break, not a 'day off' celebrated by watching two games of junior football and one netball match in the rain. It's supposed to be a day for us to relax and do absolutely nothing, but it never happens, does it?

Kids' sporting groups are part of the con, trying to mark Mother's Day by making us do more, not less. My son's footy team has a Mother's Day event where the mums have to compete in a longest kick competition and even play a Mums vs Kids game. Why are dads the ones getting the day off when it's meant to be all about us? To be frank, turning up at an oval at 9 am, being judged on my ability to look good in a pair of 2XU compression pants tighter than they used to be and trying to kick a goal while being tackled by a five-year-old is not my idea of a good time.

This day of rest often goes out the window before dawn. The kids are so excited to hand over the macaroni necklace and eggshell photo frame they've been making for weeks that they peel back mum's eyelids at 6 am and jump under the doona. The pasta necklace she will proudly wear all day is tangible proof of their love for her. (She will throw it out a few months later when she discovers it in her jewellery box, green and smelling of mould because the teacher's aide mucked up and cooked the pasta first.)

After the present-giving, the next great Mother's Day tradition plays out: breakfast in bed. The first sign something's up is the smell of burning in the air. But who cares? Half-arsed mums love any meal they haven't had to cook, and you'll find her in raptures, even when it's pretty much inedible. 'Eggs, how did you know I love them so hard?', 'Toast! How did you know I love it all dry and black like that?', '*MasterChef* here we come, kids!'

Half-arsed mums know they will probably saunter out to the kitchen an hour later to a scene of total chaos because the kids will have lost interest in cleaning up and will instead by playing the PS4 with their dad. 'We used the saucepans we gave you for Christmas,' they'll say proudly. 'Every single one of them.' Sigh. Never mind, it's Mother's Day. It's the thought that counts. 'Have a break, Mum,' the kids will say. 'You can do the washing up later.'

Let me assure you, most mums would be happy with a half-price petrol-station bunch of flowers, a handmade card and a sleep-in. Marketing to Mums surveyed 400 mothers and found they don't want products and presents for Mother's Day, but a sit-down meal with the family and for the kids not to argue. One mum said she wanted a gift that acknowledged her role as a 'unique human being' but would settle for 'a cup of tea and marmalade toast'. Another said she just wanted the kids to 'put their Zooper Dooper wrappers and the scissors away'.

Mums don't want to receive vegetable spiralisers, electronic slippers that massage their feet or magnified beauty mirrors that will make their pores look the size of pork pies. Mother's Day marketers may be surprised to know women don't spend their whole lives cleaning, cooking for others and keeping our feet warm and electronically stimulated. It reminds me of a Jenny Craig campaign a few years ago advising people to talk to their mum on Mother's Day about her weight. Dietician Karen Inge suggested it was 'a good day to consider weight because being overweight and obese puts you at major risk of disease'. Yup. Good luck with that one. Do you do that before or after the pavlova and cream?

I say, get creative, people. Head to the internet and get your lovely mum a wine glass that attaches to the top of a wine bottle, allowing her to drink without interruption. Unless she can use it, drink it, wear it or return it for something she really wants, she's not likely to be interested. A bottle of nice champers will hit the spot for most half-arsed mums. After all, kids are the reason most of us drink.

Father's Day

Dads in Father's Day ads are often portrayed as smelly drunk slackers with dirty cars who like burning things, sleeping outdoors, brewing their own alcohol and letting one rip. It's not fair. Mothers get flowers, chocolates and plug-in foot massagers to reward them for doing everything so well. Fathers get barbecue tongs, cordless drills and aprons with slogans making fun of their inability to perform household tasks (*Stand clear, man cooking!*).

Half-arsed dads are also sick of presents that help them take everyday chores to a new level, such as electric nose-hair trimmers and tongue scrapers. Where's the fun in any of that? Nothing says, 'I don't love you enough' like a tongue-scraper, even if it is the gold standard for halitosis treatment. One company is offering 'Dads at the mercy of questionable gifting' a chance to exchange 'sh*t socks' for a bottle of Fireball whiskey. It's billed as a chance for 'dad's who aren't boring f*ckers to ditch their feet warmers for a heart warmer'. Pity they don't care about dads at the mercy of questionable apostrophe use.

Retailers do their best to help the family of DIY Dad, Entertainer Dad, Tech Dad and Gardener Dad choose gifts. But where are the gifts for Slacker Dad – jumbo packs of Cheezels, trackie pants with very loose elastic and *The Simpsons* boxed DVD sets? Or what about Dorky Dad – black Explorer socks, stonewashed jeans, Barry Manilow CDs? Or Vintage Dad – old copies of *National Geographic*, velour zip-up Hush Puppies, dandruff shampoo?

Half-arsed dads draw inspiration from one survey which found 40 per cent of Aussie men say being told 'I love you' is their number one gift for Father's Day. Hugs and saying 'I love you' aren't as practical as beard strainers or tongue cleaners, but they've got advantages over everything else. They're free, you don't need to order them in advance and you don't have to pay for delivery. And they're returnable – if you give a hug, you'll get one back. Half-arsed fathers also don't rate gift cards, as they merely prove their family doesn't know them well enough to buy them real presents. Sneaky kids also know that the more generic the voucher, the greater the chance it will be used on them as the use-by date nears.

For what it's worth, here's my half-arsed Father's Day gift advice. Make sure you don't offend with gifts such as a voucher for a back wax, deodorant (even if it's disguised as body spray) or a set of bathroom scales. Don't raise his expectations and take him for a ride in a Lamborghini. He'll be the happiest dad in the world until he realises you only spent $99 not $399,000 and he has to give it back 45 minutes later. And make sure you consult with your siblings over gift choices. Some lucky dads might get both a circular-saw set and a few good bottles of red. Just make sure he doesn't use both at the same time and take his arm off while sawing under the influence.

PART THREE

Half-Arsed Solutions

Chapter 14

HALF-ARSED KIDS

Half-arsed parents want to do things differently. I haven't quite nailed it, but I try to let my kids be free by not over-scheduling every second of the day. I let them hurt themselves and do silly things like I did as a kid, such as using my sleeping bag to slide off the tin shed roof. (It wasn't my finest hour, and I had a ripped sleeping bag for the next decade.) I take my kids to the pool and let them stay all day until their hair goes green and their fingers are wrinkled. I let them go to friends' houses in the school holidays and pick them up two days later just before they are reported as missing persons. I repay the favour and have their friends to stay so long I forget they're not mine.

I leave my older kids in the car for five minutes outside a shop if it's convenient. I have faith in their survival instincts and leave them home alone. I trust them to run if the house catches fire (it probably won't) or hide if there's a burglar (there probably won't be). I let them go to the local shops and library alone, ride their bikes with their friends and catch public transport.

I make sure my kids learn how to amuse themselves without electronic babysitters by dismantling the wi-fi halfway through the school holidays. I'll turn it back on when it suits me, not them. When I was growing up we had no choice but to indulge in tech-free activities. I'm drawing inspiration from these days and trusting my kids to run free and make good decisions. Do you know what? They're happier for it, and so am I. Half-arsed parents set the bar low enough so they succeed most of the time. They trust their own instincts to get it right – and sometimes wrong, but who's checking? And they embrace parenthood and its messy imperfections rather than try to be perfect. Here are some ideas to get you started.

Embrace the mess

Half-arsed parents don't stress about having a dirty car filled every weekend with grass, mud stains, teen sweat and stinky football boots. They rifle through their son's room to find an unread book they can re-gift as a last-minute birthday party present. They give the kids Weet-Bix with water every now and then because they forgot to buy milk. It tastes like crap, but they don't get worked up about it. Half-arsed parents with younger kids are the same. Their car seats and high chairs are clean, but they wouldn't pass any white-glove test. Half-arsed kids' rooms look like real rooms, not furniture showrooms. I am fed-up with the kids' rooms you see in magazines with no toys but lots of nicely arranged objects in keeping with the signature boho Scandi mid-century colour palette. Boys' rooms often feature a heavy dose of black. Yes, black. It used to be the colour of death, but now it is on-trend for kids' bedrooms. There are no toys in sight but there is 'mint three ways', a sculptural feathered headdress and artful lettering spelling out the kid's name.

These are not half-arsed rooms. Where, I want to know, are the superhero doona covers that are the bane of most stylish parents' existence? They're garish, badly made and ugly – and kids absolutely love them. Where are the tubs of toys too big to go in the cupboard? The dress-ups? The half-made Lego creations that can't be dismantled? The butt-ugly remote-controlled cars, the tribes of Barbies in various states of undress and the piles of comics and books?

Girls' rooms shown in social media posts and magazine stories are similar havens of good taste and style, in a restrained pastel colour palette with upholstered furniture and hand-tufted carpet. There's no Disney pink, no baby photos and no splatter-paint pictures in sight. Rather, the wall sports a specially commissioned artwork that the owner gushes is 'soft aqua with a silver tint infusion and scatters of mint and raspberry'. Well, my daughter's room also has hints of mint and raspberry, but that's due to the food stains on the carpet. I'm happier with Blu-tacked artworks done by the kids themselves than commissioned masterpieces.

Half-arsed parents don't want any of these designer details that take a lot of time to keep clean and tidy. Minimalism is not the half-arsed way. They want big baskets of easily accessible toys rather than artful displays of breakables, kids' artwork over pricey prints and floorboards over white rugs. They have hand-me-down cots and change tables which are basic and functional rather than precious heirlooms. Above all, they have kids' rooms that are all about the kids, and not their parents and their social media following. Embracing messy imperfection rather than insisting on matchy-matchy kids' rooms is a key half-arsed goal. Relax, and who knows? You might even find time to clean the car and buy milk.

Vegemite pasta and other half-arsed dinners

There's a lot of parenting advice about the importance of long family dinners full of mindful intergenerational bonding, screen-free discussions and superfood rainbow bowls. But it won't always be possible, or even desirable, to manage this night after night. Luckily, some experts now say parents should abandon the goal of harmonious nightly family dinners and accept the impact of busy children, work schedules and picky eaters.

Dr Julie Green, executive director of the Raising Children Network, advises parents to keep family meals to no more than half an hour, have family breakfasts or lunches instead, and put popular, healthy dishes on high rotation to save time. 'Repetition is okay as long as it's healthy food. Create your own traditions of Monday meatballs, or Tuesday tacos,' she says. How good does that sound?

Some of my friends take a similar tack. Rather than making dinner a stressful major production, they fill their children up with healthy food during the day instead. I've even got one pal whose mid-week go-to is Vegemite pasta. It's almost entirely lacking in any nutritional value but the kids LOVE it. TV presenter and author Sonya Karras says rice, a tin of tuna and a handful of spinach leaves is her easy dinner stand-by. Mine is UberEats. Just kidding. Risotto with chicken stock cubes, parmesan from the back of the fridge and frozen peas is my go-to meal for busy weeknights when I haven't been to the supermarket. If the kids are lucky, it will be topped with a handful of spinach leaves that haven't gone slimy yet.

In my house we often play an amusing game called My Kitchen Doesn't Rule. The contestants are tired parents who do a days' work before they get home and have to cook dinner for the judges, who are their grumpy, picky children. The contestants have to find ingredients from the bottom of the veggie crisper, throwing out anything mouldy as they go. They can also select items from the back of the freezer or pantry, and get bonus points for using food that's past its use-by-date but still okay to eat.

The judges all have different dietary demands and tastes, and want to eat at different times of the evening. At the end, the contestants will pour themselves a very large glass of wine and retire to the couch, where they will spend the rest of the evening ignoring the mess in the kitchen and watching reality TV shows about other people's inept cooking efforts.

When it comes to mealtimes, doing what works for you and your family is the most important thing. Bugger what anyone else thinks. For example, I'm not a fan of kids being given phones and tablets in restaurants. I figure if you're spending the money to eat out, you may as well interact with each other. But other families with complicated schedules or kids with special needs see it differently and find screens make eating out possible – even pleasurable.

Dr Hilary Davis from Swinburne University filmed four families while they dined at four different family-friendly restaurants in order to see what happened when kids were allowed to use technology at the table. She found children put their devices away when their meals arrived and got back on them when they finished eating. Dr Davis says children were careful not to knock over dishes, drinks and cutlery and 'continued to talk and converse even though they might be in different technologies, different worlds, or realms within the games on technology ... It was apparent that families were conscious of fellow diners, e.g. parents often tell children to "quiet down" as other diners are nearby.'

So don't stress if dinner is tinned tuna or Vegemite pasta and eating out involves kids on iPads. As *Sh*tty Mum* puts it, 'I can finally take my kids to a restaurant, thank you Angry Birds!'

Let them play

Another key aspect of half-arsed parenting is giving kids time to play. My kids only do one sport or activity at a time. This leaves them time to ride bikes, scoot around the suburb and, yes, spend time on screens. I'm not saying I've got it all worked out by any means, and they probably still spend too much time playing computer games and not enough riding bikes, but at least they're not scheduled every second of the day.

A study from Deakin University found informal physical activities like paddling, climbing, skating, scooting and riding bikes have a great spin-off – they spur kids on to try other active pursuits. 'Young children think that having a go makes them better at it. While there is value in organised sport, there is also great value in doing different things in a fun context – unstructured play on a bike or climbing in the backyard,' author Dr Lisa Barnett says.

Taking kids to the park is another good antidote to scheduled activities. Queensland researchers found that when parents take kids to the park, they generally sit back and let kids decide what they want to do. As long as kids are safe, parents let them do what they liked. How very half-arsed. The best parks have equipment that lets kids take risks, with features such as lakes, dog off-leash areas, running water or trails. Kids love things like obstacle courses, mazes, flying foxes and pedal-powered trains which encourage them to be active without even realising it. This, let me assure you, is the ultimate goal. Maximum output, minimum effort – that's the half-arsed way.

Another type of play is roughhousing, a form of adventurous horseplay. My sister and I were more likely to play shops or schools than wrestle and have pillow fights. But as the mother of two boys, I quickly got up to speed with rough play. A book called *The Art of Roughhousing* says children benefit from active, physical play that teaches them self-control, fairness and empathy – and how to make swords out of any household object. Half-arsed parents love dirty, silly, rough play. That's how we ended up with kids in the first place.

Sometimes, half-arsed parents want to join in and play with their kids. I love a book called *Family, Food and Feelings* by Kate Berry, founder of the wonderful Lunch Lady blog. Berry, the mother of two girls, is useless at craft, thinks housework is boring and prefers road trips over resorts. She urges parents to keep their sense of adventure and do more fun stuff with their kids. 'It breaks my heart when people give themselves away when they have kids,' she says. 'Adventure can happen anywhere. If you're doing something you don't usually do, that's adventurous, isn't it? It might be going for a drive somewhere new, roller skating at home or even just giving your kids a midweek "good times break" by toasting marshmallows or eating ice-cream sundaes,' Berry says. Half-arsed parents like the idea of good times breaks, especially if triple-choc fudge brownie ice cream is involved.

Berry also suggests parents take children to non-kid things like rock concerts and festivals. I love this idea. 'When I was a kid my mum took me to see crazy rock acts like AC/DC and Jimmy Barnes. It means I got to know who she is,' she says. The *I Was a Good Mom Before I had Kids* ladies want parents to go on adventures too. They ask: when was the last time you enjoyed a kids' birthday party without taking photos? Played hooky to go to the movies? Declared a day for wearing pyjamas and staying home? Half-arsed parents approve of family outings based around things they want to do, not just their kids.

Let them get bored. Sooooo booooored.

During the Covid lockdowns, wi-fi outages and narky parents demanding they 'put that bloody screen away' tested many kids' capacity for self-directed, unplugged entertainment. Kids don't know how lucky they are thanks to the 24-hour cartoon channel, superhero-themed underpants and cheap overseas holidays. When I was a kid, we only got *The Curiosity Show* on Saturday mornings, wore plain old undies and spent holidays driving across the Nullarbor in the backseat of an unairconditioned Kingswood, frying our legs on the vinyl seats. There were no iPads, just endless games of 'I Spy' and the excitement of spotting iconic Australian animals as roadkill on the side of the highway. We got bored and made up silly games to pass the time, like having competitions over who could eat a packet of chips the slowest.

My kids don't know anything about boredom. Every school holidays, I crack the irrits and make them turn off their screens and then they spend the rest of the day complaining they're bored. 'I'm boooored,' they report glumly every five seconds. It happened the other day and the results weren't pretty. Although it was sunny and we have a house full of toys and games, the kids immediately complained they had 'nothing to do'. They would have been happy if I had taken them to the park or started a game of driveway basketball. But I had work to do. I needed them to entertain themselves. They were genuinely stumped when challenged to amuse themselves for an hour or two without electronic or parental help.

Experts say it usually takes kids about 20 minutes to settle down and find a game or something else to do. Boys are worse than girls, and my son took half an hour to find something to do (bounce a ball against the side of the house) while my daughter settled down to ~~burn~~ cook some cakes. As you know, I'm not one of those parents advocating a complete ban on screens or scheduled activities, but at times, kids need to come up with things to do that don't involve screens. In fact, experts say it's good for kids to be bored as it fuels creativity and problem-solving.

'Boredom teaches children to push themselves, boosts resilience and helps contribute to positive self-esteem,' Dr Julie Green from the Parenting Research Centre says. 'Parents often feel as if they have to entertain their kids all the time, but they don't. Children benefit from working out what to do with themselves. They can explore ideas and do something that matches their mood. It's a fantastic catalyst for kids using their imagination and creating different play scenarios.' As the *Sh*tty Mums* remind us, boredom is character-building. 'How else will your older child figure out how hard she needs to pinch your youngest child before she cries?' As they explain, 'It's the bored child who will discover that boogers are salty, Sharpies work as well on walls as they do on paper, and that a steady hand can tease the legs off a living fly.'

It's great advice for half-arsed parents who think kids should play by themselves rather than be entertained all the time. But it's not always possible. There's a time to reap, a time to sow, a time to play and a time to be dumped in front of the electronic babysitter because mum or dad has work to do. And that's fine too.

Go camping. Yes, even you.

Research shows camping makes kids more resilient, more confident, less anxious and less stressed. So what's stopping you? Just kidding. Lucky for you, I am not suggesting half-arsed parents should pack up the two-man tent and go bush. That would be hypocritical given that the last time I went camping was in 1979. A tent pitched in the backyard is a perfect half-arsed solution. It's different, fun and close to wi-fi and bottle shops.

I remember trying to put up a tent someone sent me because they wanted me to write about how much fun camping was. What a joke. I struggled for well over an hour to erect a pretty basic tent. In the end, it looked like a large pair of underpants billowing on a patch of grass. There were 15 pegs and two poles left over, and my daughter, who was then only ten, could barely squeeze in the opening by crawling on her side. Then my dad stepped in to help, and re-erected the damned thing in about five minutes without putting down his stubby of beer.

We stocked up on gadgets – a campfire cooker (useless), a padded esky (essential) and a battery light hung from the tent ceiling (cute and nifty). What surprised me was how much the kids loved huddling in the rain on tiny foam mattresses when the comfort of their bedrooms was metres away. This simple event captured the imagination of our little family. We toasted marshmallows on the tiny aluminium cooker, trying to ignore the metho taste. We sang campfire songs with dodgy lyrics until the neighbours complained. And we grabbed the dogs and cuddled in close for warmth as the temperature dropped.

The tent stayed up all summer and gave the kids something to do when I made them turn off the screens. If left to their own devices, my kids would spend the entire school holidays watching bad Adam Sandler movies on the TV while simultaneously playing Subway Surfers on their phones and stuffing their face with Happy Meals. At least the tent enabled them to do some of those things outside of the house for a change. We took it down at the end of January and the bare patch of dead grass was an enduring reminder of the Most Excellent Summer of the Tent.

Don't get me wrong. I am not trumpeting my own camping cred here. My tent may be made by Kathmandu and my sleeping bag by North Face, but neither are likely to leave my inner-city postcode anytime soon. It's a pity, because we used to go camping every weekend as a family when I was growing up in South Australia's Flinders Ranges. We'd pile everyone into the Kingswood and throw in a few essentials: an esky packed with longnecks, an army folding spade used as a dunny shovel and a few tins of baked beans and Irish Stew. If my parents were too ~~drunk~~ tired to put up the tent, we'd all sleep in the car. Easy. These days, it's more about 'glamping' thanks to pneumatic inflatable tents, squeezable water filtration systems and solar-powered lights. But who knows? Maybe next holidays we might give camping another go. We might even make it outside of our own backyard. But I doubt it. Half-arsed parents have many talents. Knowing their limits is one of them.

Leave them alone

Hyper-parents are obsessed with safety. They prefer their kids are strapped into prams and car seats rather than venture out alone. Half-arsed parents want to let kids do more things for themselves and by themselves. This is a very important goal. It gives us a break and bolsters their independence. Parenting writer Justin Coulson is a big believer in children being given freedom. He says kids in late primary school can walk to school, play unattended in a playground and ride a bike around the neighbourhood. But they should wait until high school to stay home alone at night, get a job or get a phone.

As Coulson sees it, there are many variables, but this shouldn't stop parents from trying to let their kids have as much freedom as is safe for them. 'Location, time of day, child personality and temperament, presence of friends or others (or no one), and so many other factors may mean that something can be done earlier or later,' Coulson says. For instance, when thinking about when kids can walk to school alone, Coulson suggests parents consider the distance, the number of roads that need to be crossed, safety measures and the time of day. 'It could be as young as seven, but might need to wait until at least 12 or 13,' he says.

When it comes to leaving kids alone, it depends on the situation and the child. 'Where are you going? How long will you be? Do they know how to get help? What time of day is it?' he says.

Why not start with Skenazy's vision for the local park? Remember Lenore Skenazy? She let her nine-year-old ride the subway alone. She's been urging parents to take their kids to the park – and leave without them. It's a brilliant idea. Why not take your school-aged kids to the park? Tell them to have fun, make friends and not leave with anyone else. Go off and have a coffee or do something else, and pick them up again in the allotted time, say, an hour. When that doesn't seem like a big deal, maybe move on to letting them ride their bikes, climb trees, make dinner and make friends with neighbourhood kids.

Kids should also be encouraged to become independent by doing paid and unpaid work when they are old enough. Half-arsed parents are raising their kids to be resilient and independent and pay their own way as soon as possible. Research from Yale University shows parents can lessen the impact of adverse events such as divorce, death and family violence by building their kids' skills and experiences outside of the home. This includes encouraging them to get jobs and volunteer.

Psychologist Stuart Passmore, author of *Parenting for a Happier Home,* also wants kids to do more chores around the house. 'Giving children simple chores teaches them responsibility and respect,' he says. 'Even a two-year-old can put toys away.' Half-arsed parents heartily endorse this approach. If they can put small objects up their nose or down the toilet, then surely they can put them away too. The more chores, the better. Dr Melissa Olfert from West Virginia University says parents are put off getting kids to help by a lack of time and concern for their safety. But she found kids love the idea of doing things like cooking meals. Children embrace the idea because they 'need to know how to cook later in life'. Dr Olfert says children want their parents to demonstrate skills, select age-appropriate tasks for them and reward them for helping. Sounds like a win–win, as long as no one gets hurt and nothing burns down.

Let's hope your kids will be more co-ordinated than a certain teenager I know who sliced his shin open with an axe when he did chores at his cousin's country property. And don't listen when the kids try and tell you no one does jobs at home anymore. The Family Values report shows kids under 18 get around $15 a week in exchange for washing the dishes, cleaning their bedrooms and doing the laundry. Overall, 43 per cent of kids do chores in exchange for pocket money. Remember that figure when your kids roll their eyes and tell you doing jobs is 'so last century'.

Ignore bad advice

Half-arsed parents also back themselves and ignore crappy advice that doesn't feel right. Social researcher Neer Korn found first-time parents are petrified of doing the wrong thing, but when they look back, they wish they'd had the confidence to back themselves. By the time the second child arrives, they're more chilled, but still find it hard to let go and trust their gut instincts. It's a pity because, in most cases, parents know for themselves the right thing to do.

A few years ago, I did a story about a book on anxious kids. The author suggested parents be present, ditch digital devices, do one thing at a time and set aside one-on-one time with their kids. It shows how out-of-touch most parenting advice is – parents can

NEVER do one thing at a time, or ditch the mobile phone once they're home. Multitasking and mobile phones make it possible for most parents to get through a busy evening. No wonder parents are feeling bad – the so-called experts meant to help us are setting the bar so high no one can live up to their rules.

As a case in point, the other night I was cooking seafood marinara with separate salmon for one child who doesn't like pasta. While I was stirring, I was helping my son think of rhymes about simple machines, levers and wheels, I was helping my daughter fill in camp medical forms by trying to work out dates she'd had vaccinations and I was on hold with my bank because I needed to cancel my credit card. Just another night in the O'Brien household. One of the rhymes about levers was, 'Wheels need axles to make them go, without that, they'd be much more slow.' Okay, I didn't say I was doing any of these things well, did I?

I shouldn't be surprised about the bad suggestions parents are offered. I did a story a few years ago about all the bizarre, outdated and inaccurate advice new parents are given by family and friends. For instance, parents are being told to give newborns herbal tea, let the pets babysit and teach kids a lesson by 'biting them back'. Much of the advice from their parents was 30 years out of date and 'didn't always reflect the new research', according to the head of the national Pregnancy, Birth and Baby hotline. No kidding.

Half-arsed parents go with the flow, and I mean their flow, not half-baked, sanctimonious crap served up by those who want kids not to be anxious but don't give a damn about anxious adults. It's not as hard as it sounds.

Chapter 15

HALF-ARSED HEROES

Many of those offering advice to other mums and dads are uptight hyper-parents or natural nutcases raising children aided by the celestial power of organic rainbow unicorn crystals. Half-arsed parents have mastered the art of keeping it real. They're down-to-earth and not afraid to admit when they get it wrong. They're also a great antidote to the Insta-scammers and Fakebookers keen to show off their shiny, perfect lives. All of my favourite half-arsed heroes are Australian. Perhaps this is because the half-arsed approach reflects the laidback Aussie way of life.

TV and radio host Carrie Bickmore is a key half-arsed hero. She keeps her social media feed full of honest depictions of her life as a working mum with three kids. In one post, she's lying on a couch dozing under a chic hat, her cute little newborn nestled contentedly in her arms. Swipe right and gone is the artful posing, the filter and the cropping. A second photo, taken from a very unflattering angle, makes her looks like any other exhausted new parent crashed out on a sofa. Bickmore, who's gorgeous, funny and clever, has gone out of her way to tell others how she's found raising Oliver, Evie and Adelaide to be tough at times, particularly after the death of Oliver's father.

She's written about the sleepless nights, anxiety, sleep deprivation, miscarriages and reflux, and received heaps of sympathy. And yet, even Bickmore faced judgment over her decision to let her nine-year-old walk to school alone. 'I thought I was sharing a trivial anecdote about my son's new-found independence, as part of a conversation about helicopter parenting. But I had opened a can of nasty worms. People went out of their way to tell me nine is too young for a kid to walk to school, and I was negligent for not calling to check he'd made it safely,' Bickmore writes in *Stellar* magazine. She wants parents to give each other a break. 'I am a working mum, just like mine was,' she says. 'Occasionally I'll miss things. Things might be forgotten. But that's okay. When it comes to our time together, it is quality not quantity.'

It's a great half-arsed maxim: assume things are fine unless you hear otherwise. Another mum taking a similar approach is radio host Fifi Box. Box, a single mother of two young girls, is candid about serving UberEats for dinner and dealing with crazy work hours and intense media intrusion. She even posted a photo of her newborn daughter pooing on her arm. Author Zoe Foster Blake agrees that trying to do it all is 'a bad idea'. Foster Blake posted a photo of her new office on social media recently, saying she's figured out that working from home means she does 'neither parenting, nor work, very well'. She says she got the office in order to 'leave behind the staccato, unfocused, half-arsed half-worker half-parent I currently am'. Sounds familiar, especially the half-arsed, half-worker, half-parent bit.

Here are some other half-arsed heroes.

Jessica Rowe

Jessica Rowe has been on Australian TV screens for years. Funny, self-deprecating and witty, her motto is comedian Phyllis Diller's famous quote: 'Housework won't kill you, but why take the chance?' In her latest book, she explains she's a proud 'crap housewife'. 'It's my way of being light-hearted so I can take the pressure off myself and realise I am good enough,' she says. 'Part of that vulnerability has meant letting go of the apron strings tied around the airbrushed image of what a family is "supposed" to look like,' she writes. 'Sometimes this means I feed my tribe toast for dinner.' Sunday means baked beans for dinner and on Monday it's sausages 'in varying states of charcoal'. 'Okay I am a crappy cook and messy "housekeeper" but that doesn't matter. There are plenty of other things I am good at,' Rowe says. The list includes loving her family, being a loyal friend, a good daughter and wearing glittery eyeliner.

As Rowe writes, her wish is that 'you can find some sparkle, light and sprinklings of fairy dust as you navigate your own not-so-perfect but glorious life!' Sounds good to me. Besides, what's not to like about a woman who shares her nightly dinner recipes for those who don't like to cook but have a family who likes to eat?

Rowe, like other half-arsed parents, has learnt to be more gentle with herself. As she explains in her book, she hated the mind-numbing grind of playgrounds, but thought that's what she had to do to be a good mum. Now she's a self-professed good enough mum who spends her time doing things that are fun for her too – like dress-ups, colouring in and listening to the birdsong of local magpies.

Her philosophy is one worth adopting. 'Do whatever gets you through that moment, day or night.' She's also learnt to pick her battles. 'It doesn't matter if they don't want to brush their hair, wear the same outfit or eat the same food for weeks on end. But I won't tolerate rudeness or bad manners.' I wish more parents felt the same way.

Madeleine West

Madeleine West, actor and author, at one stage had six kids under the age of eight with chef Shannon Bennett. That's right. Six children. West is a great example of a half-arsed parent. She may have been on *Neighbours* and had a song recorded by Paris Hilton, but she also once found her toddler eating dog biscuits. She breastfed her twins on the toilet to save time. And when she's in crisis mode, she throws Nutri-Grain over the floor and locks the doors. In her 2016 book *Six Under Eight: When Mothering Becomes an Extreme Sport*, she describes life in 'Chateau Catastrophe' in all of its crazy glory. There are stories about being on the side of the freeway with her breast hanging out after a maternity bra malfunction, and one child falling off a balcony onto a wooden floor. It's not perfect, but it is honest. It's no wonder she also writes, 'Beside gin and valium, online shopping is a mother's best friend.'

West's stories are a terrific reminder that half-arsed parents don't have to be obsessed with their offspring. If fact, it's better for everyone if they're not. However, there's one thing I can't agree with her on. 'If you return home from the school drop-off and all the beds aren't made, that will automatically ruin your harmony,' she says. It doesn't work like that in my house. If I return home from school drop-off and the beds *are* made, it means an intruder's been in my house.

Mia Freedman

Publisher and founder of website Mamamia, Mia Freedman became editor of *Cosmopolitan* magazine at 24 and had a baby nine months later. Years later, her son, Luca Lavigne, wrote about life with a busy – and chronically disorganised – mum. Mia invited Luca to pen a chapter for her book *Work, Strife, Balance* and he responded by detailing how he had to organise his own lifts to parties, didn't have a present to give the birthday child and worried she wouldn't be there to pick him up. Freedman managed a staff of 70 but would forget to pick him up from after-school care.

More recently, Freedman wrote about her younger son Remy going through the same thing. She was travelling and forgot to order his school lunch online. 'Those kinds of details I don't remember, and then part of me thinks it helps them be resilient, because of course he was fine, he went to the tuckshop and they gave him a cheese sandwich,' she told *Stellar* magazine recently. Half-arsed parents don't see it as a badge of honour not to remember these things, but nor do they see it as a personal failing or a cause for catastrophe if they do. And they teach kids how to order their own damned lunches.

Freedman knows she's not great with the little things, but she's done a lot right. She's raised her kids to be curious, empathetic and articulate. She's shown them the benefits of having a strong work ethic and professional goals, even though this got in the way of her parenting at times. And she's shown them life isn't always about them. Anyone who's had the confidence to write a book called *Mama Mia: Mistakes, Magazines and Motherhood* is a half-arsed hero, for sure.

Shannon Kelly White

Another mothering superstar is Shannon Kelly White, a Victorian mother of two young boys and blogger at Shannon's Kitchen. Her book *Parenting for Legends* urges mums and dads to surrender to survival mode, be lazy where possible, accept help and be kind to themselves. 'These days it feels like parenting is a competitive sport with everyone trying to outdo each other trying to be "the perfect parent". Well, bugger that. Kids don't need us to be perfect, they just need us to be kind and loving,' she writes.

A former nurse who lives in Torquay with her husband Brett, a computer game designer, White says her skills include wearing Reebok pumps, eating cookies and making zoos out of Duplo. She says she has enjoyed having kids. 'I decided not to try and be perfect. Some days I nail it and some days are sh*thouse,' she says. 'You might be tempted to show off and prove to the world that you can do it all, but really, the world doesn't particularly care so you might as well calm down.'

White says it's more important to maintain friendships and stay sane than have a perfect house. 'Reasonable people will accept that you're currently time poor and they won't care if you have tumbleweeds of human hair rolling idly down your hallway,' she writes. 'So don't let your untidy house stop you socialising! Just pop a bra on, crack a window and say: "Come on in, friends".' Chapters in her book include: 'Pre-schoolers are know-nothing know-it-alls' and 'Sometimes at night you want to put them in the bin'. But White wants readers to know that she has 'had children for almost six years and has never put them in the bin, not even once'.

These women are half-arsed, but only when it doesn't matter. The kids are loved and safe, so who cares if their houses are a bit messy and they only wear bras when they've got company?

Half-arsed dads

There are plenty of half-arsed hero dads out there too. One is Melbourne stay-at-home dad Clint Greagen, who calls himself the 'bogan Anthony Robbins' and 'a guy with a strong aversion to actual paid work'. As Greagen says, he's surrounded by people who think he's just a 'funny man who hangs out washing like a lady'. His book, *Reservoir Dad*, is filled with stories about toilet paper snakes, snot mopping, chasing a chicken called Tandoori and wiping up urine in public places with the *Footy Record*. As he sees it, 'there's certainly not enough appreciation of how hard it is to be at home with kids full-time, and how important it is. That's true whether you're a dad or a mum.' 'You do need to keep your sense of humour as a survival mechanism, even if it has been a terrible day,' he says.

In the US, comedian Chris Illuminati offers a similarly humorous – even illuminating – view of daddy day care. He started by writing notes to remind himself what to do when caring for his children Evan, four, and Lyla, nine months, and is now an internet sensation. 'Woke up at 3 am to find kid crying and covered in vomit. Had to clean him and clothes and bed. And they said I wouldn't learn anything from being in a fraternity,' one note says. And another: 'Bought the kid a training potty. He sat down on it and pretended to talk on the phone. No comment on where he learnt that from.' It reminds me of *Hear Me Roar*, a great book written by Aussie stay-at-home dad Ben Robertson. As his son put it one day, 'Mummy's going off to work. You're going nowhere.'

More half-arsed dads feature in a Bonds Baby Search clip made a few years ago. The dads, comedian Dave Hughes, radio presenter Ryan 'Fitzy' Fitzgerald and tennis champ Pat Rafter, offer a refreshing take on half-arsed fatherhood. The clip opens with Rafter optimistically inviting his mates and their babies over to watch the cricket. After a play outside, it's lunchtime and they move the table to make way for a trio of highchairs sitting on a tarpaulin on the floor. Brilliant idea. Afterwards, they pin the tarp to the clothesline and hose it down, along with the kids' clothing. 'Who says men can't multitask?' Hughesy says, as Fitzy aims the hose at Pat. A nappy-changing competition follows. Perhaps for the first time ever, a man is shown changing a nappy without snide jokes being made. The day is nearly done by the time the cricket's turned on, and they sit there, rocking the prams quietly. Then a wicket is lost, and they wake the babies up with their yells. Even this isn't a catastrophe and they agree to 'walk it off' in a nearby park. At the end of the day, the guys joke about one baby being 'hosed down like a 4WD' and another being given a 'blow dry with a vacuum cleaner'.

It's no doubt scripted, but it still rings true. Half-arsed dads, like half-arsed mums, are problem-solvers who don't worry about what others may think. They get the job done with practical solutions and minimum angst. I've never dried a child with a vacuum cleaner, but why the hell not? Who knows? I might end up with a clean floor, which would be a bonus.

Chapter 16

HALF-ARSED
HAPPINESS

Half-arsed parents want satisfaction on their own terms, in their
own way. It doesn't always have to be about the kids. They know
they matter too. They know their friends and parents – if they're
lucky enough to still have them around – matter too. Freed from
obsessing about their children's progress and commitments, half-
arsed parents have the time and energy to nurture their relationships.
They do less, which enables them to give more to others. This not
only makes them better people, but better parents as well.

Half-arsed parents think happiness is important. They don't
listen to people who tell them that happiness is all about finding
inner peace. Or 'failing is winning' or 'inspire yourself with you'.
Half-arsed parents are more inspired by winning $20 million in
the lottery and finding their son's lost soccer boots in the school's
lost property bin.

There are many reasons half-arsed parents are happy. It's about
appreciating simple everyday things, rejecting unrealistic role

models and keeping the kids' demands in check. Half-arsed parents look after themselves the same way they look after everyone else. I remember my daughter doing kindergarten dancing or tots 'n' tutus or something awful like that many years ago. They had a 'Mum and Me' presentation day where the mothers and daughters went on stage together. Mothers were instructed to 'wear all black, that way you will not stand out and allow the children to take the limelight!' That's modern motherhood: you pay an extra $50 for the privilege of making sure no one can see you in the background. Dads are treated much worse; some fathers have to fight for the right to go backstage at their kids' concerts at all. It's time to channel *Dirty Dancing* and make sure no one keeps half-arsed parents in the corner.

Here's some suggestions about the things that matter to half-arsed parents – baking from scratch at midnight doesn't come close. Half-arsed parents make time for old friends and new friends. They are also kind rather than critical.

Old friends

Your new baby won't sleep. Your toddler is having a meltdown. Your teens are driving you cray-cray. This is a time for old friends. Old friends stretching back to childhood are the keepers of deep, dark secrets. They know all the dirt – from your little incident in the prep playground that led to the police being called to the first pash you had at a Blue Light Disco back in the 80s.

Old female friends tell each other vital things no one else will – like the fact that someone has missed a huge patch in the middle of their back with the fake tan, or that the white jeans they're wearing are totally see-through, and not in a good way. Male friendships are important too. Some men like a heart-to-heart. Others bond by handing a beer to a mate, turning on a TV screen and cheering in sync.

Old friends help choose new hairstyles, gently steering their mates away from getting an asymmetrical buzz cut with a pink rat's tail. Old friends don't tell each other they look fat. Ever. But they always notice when someone has lost weight. And they always tell their friends they're great dancers, like John Travolta in *Saturday Night Fever* rather than Elaine from *Seinfeld*.

Old friends don't tease each other about having a crush on Elton John when they were 10, loving George Michael at 15 and wanting to marry Ricky Martin at 25. They are there after a nasty breakup when someone needs to get drunk and look up old flames on Facebook. They steer them away from stalking on LinkedIn, which lets premium subscribers know who's been checking them out.

Contact may wax and wane over the years, but old friends always keep in touch. When I got divorced a few years ago, I relied on my old friends more than ever, and I always make time for them now. I now have a wonderful new partner, and my friends have embraced him and his kids too. Half-arsed parents know their old friends can be counted on: they know when to leave them alone, send a text, drop by or leave a chicken pie on their doorstep.

New friends

If the idea of hanging out with old friends who know all your secrets makes you break out in a cold sweat, never fear. New friends are here. Half-arsed parents know it's important to have mummy or daddy friends too. A dear friend and footy mum Tania Thomas used to say that 'your vibe attracts your tribe'. She was right. She had breast cancer for many years and knew more than most what was important in life. Give out welcoming vibes, and you'll attract the same kind of people back to you. Becoming a parent means there's a whole new mob out there waiting for you.

Lauren Dubois's book *You Will (Probably) Survive* details the importance of finding mates. She advises women to be friends with down-to-earth mums, chilled mums and funny mums. But she suggests steering clear of expert mums, mums you need to impress and competitive mums. As she writes, 'No one needs the added pressure of someone sweetly and innocently asking you, "Oh, isn't Rufus rolling yet? Goodness, Milo was rolling weeks ago! I think he's just extra-strong, you know?" What you need is the mum who's going to say, "Yeah, Cooper's rolling but he hasn't found his hands, so I probably won't contact the AIS just yet".' Right on, sister.

Here are some other friends to make up your tribe.

Mothers' groups

A great source of friendship for women are mothers' groups. Local councils connect mums in their area who give birth around the same time. Author and radio host Libbi Gorr explains this process in her mothering manual *The A–Z of Mummy Manners: An Etiquette Guide for Managing Other Children's Mothers and Assorted Mummy Dilemmas*. 'Becoming a mum, you end up making a whole new group of friends, most of which have been chosen for you by your child who is under five. This means, sadly, that you may not have anything else in common with the other Mummy other than the fact you have chosen to breed.' (Gorr's great book includes topics such as Tupperware etiquette, Zoloft and not being a domestic goddess. 'Face it, sister, you weren't bred to bake. Own it. Get your PhD. Move on,' she writes.)

Maybe that's why mothers' groups can be a tough gig. Half-arsed parents know they might get a whole lot of wonderful, chilled, fun mums, or a pack of mean-girl mums judging them on their bed hair, bottle-feeding and elastic-waisted pants. This was the experience of author and *Lunch Lady* mum Kate Berry. 'I was the only mum at mothers' group who didn't breastfeed and I didn't go back,' Berry says. 'The other mums looked like they were doing it with ease and I was so envious.' Fifteen years on, she knows better. 'If you dig deeper you see it's not how they see themselves at all. You need to be a bit nicer to everyone and yourself.' She's right. Half-arsed parents know the ones trying the hardest to impress them are the ones who are probably struggling the most.

In some places, mothers' groups are becoming parenting groups because more fathers are primary carers. This is great; many dads at home with young kids are more isolated as there's so few of them. Fathers need friends too, especially if they're the only male at school pick-up surrounded by women talking about heavy period flows.

I met my mothers' group mums 16 years ago and still see two of them a few times a year for dinner. We remember birthdays and Christmas presents, although sometimes we take too long to get organised and end up bringing a year's worth of presents to our catch-up. The best thing is that our sons are all exactly the same age, so it's great to compare what stage they're up to. Once it was all about nappies and naps, now we're pulling out reading glasses to read the menu and saying to each other, 'Is it me or is it hot in here?'.

Online group friends

If your old friends haven't adjusted to the fact that you are now a parent and deserve their admiration and respect, move on! Find your tribe another way. These days, social media forums bring together all sorts of weird and wonderful people. One is a national group called Mums Who Wine. It involves local businesses hosting groups of mums at events and making them feel like VIPs for a night. Isn't that a great idea? If you're feeling a bit isolated and want a whine and a wine, then head online.

There's a whole world of other parenting groups out there waiting for half-arsed pals: online playgroup mums, dads who live in the northern suburbs, mums who are still breastfeeding kids in primary school, dads who love gin, mums who had miscarriages, dads who go camping, mums who hate camping and everyone else in between. Websites such as Kidspot, Essential Baby, Bub Hub and Mamamia also offer great chances for parents to come together and ~~bitch~~ share stories through forums and discussion pages.

School parents

Other great half-arsed pals are preschool and school parents. If you can juggle work or sleeping toddlers, it's a great idea to hang out at the school or kindergarten for a few minutes at drop-off and pick-up time. The mums and dads you chat to are likely to be your tribe for the next decade or more. You'll find having kids the same age is a great reason to begin a new friendship. Start with a coffee but I'll bet you'll be swilling champers or beer on a Friday arvo before you know it.

Most of my closest friends are women I met through my kids' school. I remember my anxiety when my older son started at our local primary school. I was happy (very happy) he was starting school, but intimidated about getting to know a whole new batch of people. Luckily, I met some awesome ladies and blokes. Over the years we've shared rides, done emergency pick-ups and drop-offs, babysat each other's kids and knocked back more than a few bottles of bubbly. Our prep group of six couples has been through four divorces and one suicide in the ten years we've been friends. Only one couple in the group is still together. It hasn't been easy, but we've been there for each other and still catch up regularly.

In lockdown we had a few online catch-ups on Zoom. There was always someone who couldn't get it all to work. 'Can you hear me?' 'TURN ON YOUR MICROPHONE!!!' (Gotta love Zoom – why have one chin when you can have three?) There's nothing like a bunch of middle-aged women drinking champagne while they ignore their children fighting at top volume in the background about who ate all the Doritos. Actually, we had to scale back our Zooms because it's hard to cook dinner when you're intoxicated.

Take the time to find your tribe and invest in these friendships. In the end, it doesn't matter where you met or how long you've known each other. Find some other half-arsed parents who don't judge you for licking a dirty dummy and ramming it straight back in a baby's mouth, or pretending the swing is broken because you can't face another pushing session at the playground. Half-arsed parents make great mates and they're always happy to bond with people with lower standards than them.

Parents matter

Being a half-arsed parent has another great spin-off: it can bring mums and dads closer to their own parents. Half-arsed parents are more relaxed and less insecure because they've stopped competing and doing things to make others happy. This means they have time to spend with their own parents. Once I became a mother, I realised what my own parents had been putting up with all these years. Let's face it, most of our parents could spend a lot of time saying, 'I told you so', but don't. They're the ones we think of every time we tell our own kids to 'Sit up and eat', lather squirming bodies with sunscreen, or say, 'You're not going out of this house dressed like that!'. The lucky ones still have our mums and dads around to be friends, not just parents.

My mum Jen rocks. She lets my sister and me call her by her first name, lent us her clothes when we were younger and knits the best jumpers ever. She follows the grandkids on Instagram, dutifully leaving messages on their posts – 'GR8!!!', she'll write on her teenage granddaughter's party snaps. I put a call out on Facebook and friends all told me how ace their mums are. There's Helen's mum who was still baking cakes at 90, Janelle's mother who once tried to give a McDonald's food order to a garbage bin and Carol's mum Lesley who 'chased the burglar out of her house with a rake'. Go Nanna Lesley! Jackie says her mum 'made wherever we were home' and Alison says her mum 'taught her to be kind, hardworking and take no shit from anyone'.

Mothers don't always behave, like one mum, who once 'put a pie in a country Vic umpire's face after a footy game. She had to appear before the tribunal in Ballarat many years ago. Lucky, she got off no charges!' Leanne describes her mum as tough and soft. 'When buying undies for a brother once she asked a shop assistant for ones with extra heavy undercarriage! (my brother requested as a joke!) Miss her every day.' Bernie also paid tribute to his mother, who died aged 91. She went from being 'single and at home at 39 and married with 8 kids at 40 and one of her own (me) the next year.' Nine kids. Gee, that sure puts all of our middle-class first-world problems into perspective, doesn't it? I'll bet Bernie's mum never once worried if the school mums judged her for wearing the same outfit two days running.

Fathers are just as awesome. My father Mick fancied himself as a humourist when we were growing up. 'Hope you got a discount for that top,' he'd say, when I'd appear in a tiny T-shirt in my teenage years. 'Looks like they only made half of it.' Like many men of his generation, he was quiet and unassuming until he'd get behind the wheel. Then he'd let rip. 'Bloody idiot,' he'd say if someone was three seconds late pulling out from the traffic lights. But he would also queue up patiently to get an old lady he didn't even know a coffee at an airport when our plane was delayed. I remember how proud I was to have a dad who did things like that. He was kind, and kindness counts for a lot.

I remember when my mum was away a few years ago and the kids and I were coming to their house in the country for the night. Three days before our arrival, an email arrived from Dad. 'What would you like me to get for dinner Friday and breakfast Sat?' he asked. I suggested something easy, like sausages or pizza. I was busy and didn't really care. 'I'll get some snags and maybe a frozen pizza. Okay?' he replied. 'Okay,' I wrote impatiently. But he wasn't finished. A few hours later, he was still thinking about it. 'Any special sort of snags or pizza they'd like?' Maybe Dad was panicking because it had been 35 years since he'd bought food for children. Or maybe he cared enough to get it right.

My friend Sue feels the same about her father, who died a few years ago. When she first moved out of home, she would pop back to see her parents on weekends. 'I'd be inside with Mum and say,

"Where's Dad?" and Mum would say, "He's out the front," and I'd look out and he'd be washing my car for me,' Sue said. 'He wouldn't say anything, he'd just do it.' Other friends have similar stories. Siobhan tells me that when she started doing a job involving early shifts, her dad 'used to set his alarm to wake me up, make me breakfast to eat in the car and in winter even go down and start my car to warm it up.'

Linda still remembers the way her father – who passed away when she was 16 – used to make time every night to ask her about her day. 'He would not accept "okay" or "fine". He wanted to really know. I will never forget that,' she says. Jules says her father always bought her a Valentine's Day card 'just in case I didn't have an admirer'. Half-arsed parents know their own parents matter a lot – and not only because they make time for babysitting on a Saturday night. They have time to nurture these relationships because they're not overly obsessed with their own kids and documenting and celebrating their minor non-achievements. They emulate the best of their own childhoods and draw inspiration from their own parents.

Same goes for siblings. They're the ones who don't let us get away with anything, but we know that if we ever need anything, they'll be there in a flash. My sister Katie is kind and wise and a wonderful auntie. She often hosts Christmas at her house by the river, is a great cook and babysits my dogs and kids. She's also nice enough not to bring up the fact that I expressed my honest opinion of her favourite girl's name 20 years ago when she was pregnant for the first time. Luckily she had a boy – two, in fact – and was smart enough not to confer with me when naming either of her sons.

Kindness matters too

Half-arsed parents give and receive kindness because they're not in a mindless race to the top. They know that when times get tough, kindness will get you by. I found this out recently after my father Mick died after a long illness. When all hope is lost and death is near, kindness means a lot. A cup of tea offered by a nurse. A family room in the hospital with a box of tissues and a phone charger. Somewhere comfortable for my mum to sleep so she wasn't parted from her husband of nearly 50 years in his last hours. A room big enough for the family to congregate in when saying goodbye for the last time. A room that was soundproof so no one could hear the family belting out my father's favourite songs as he lay there between life and death.

The Covid pandemic – when people did their bit for the country by sitting on the couch rather than going to war – bought out similarly strong emotions. I'm glad to say kindness was at the forefront, as people found new ways to connect with each other. There was the church choir leader who sang *Hallelujah* to a Covid patient from outside on the street. The kid whose friends did a drive-by past his house when he got home after finishing chemo. Nurses given a standing ovation from their families in the hallway after coming home from a long shift caring for Covid patients. The little girl delivering rainbow loom bands to her friends.

I wrote about two seven-year-old best friends called Alfred and Sam who started corresponding the old-fashioned way, via letters. Sam wrote: 'Dear Alfred, you are my best friend. You are fast and you make me larf and larf.' Alfred wrote: 'Dear Sam,

Nok Nok, whose there? Bum cow. Bum cow who? Bum cow is playing football.'

In some cases, the new feeling of community out there was not even related to the virus. During isolation, one woman I interviewed called Tarsha Andrews put up a billboard to get people to help find her beloved lost cat Minnie. In five weeks, she had more than 75 calls with possible sightings, including a woman who left chocolates on her doorstep telling her to 'hang in there'. 'Out of tragedy has come a connectedness to my local community I'd not ever felt or imagined in the two decades I've lived here,' Tarsha said.

There's no doubt kindness is desperately needed during a global pandemic – so is laughter. Did you remember the UK lady in the sparkly leotard singing her own version of *I Will Survive*? 'As long as I've got internet/I know I'll stay alive.' The clip was filmed in honour of 'all the slags in isolation wondering how the f*ck you're going to live through an indefinite number of months stuck indoors'. It made me larf and larf.

Our daily act of friendship and kindness is visiting 103-year-old Betty, who lives a few doors down from my son's school. Betty's walls are decorated with letters commemorating her 100th birthday from her local MPs, the Governor-General, the Queen, and the one she really treasures – the Carlton Football Club. Her house is largely original, with a multitude of sheds out the back, chooks and a lovely veggie garden. Once, many kids visited her. A decade ago, she'd have them lining up on her veranda. She'd mind younger siblings while mums raced up to the school gate, hand out homemade cake and have a chat.

But times have changed. People are busier and don't have as much time to sit and talk to an old lady whose hearing isn't the best. More parents stay in the airconditioned comfort of their cars. So now, my younger son is Betty's only regular visitor from the school. He plays her songs on his guitar, and tells her about his weekend plans, soccer matches, karate practice and everything else. Betty adores him and calls him her boyfriend.

A few years ago, my son told me he loved her. 'But I can't marry her,' he said.

'Why?'

'Because by the time I am 18, she'll be dead,' he said. The 92-year age gap wasn't a factor.

Half-arsed parents have freed themselves from the constraints of other people's expectations. They know celebrities may look good but are probably full of shit. They know the fanciest, best looking mum or dad in the school yard is probably as anxious as everyone else and faking it 'til they make it. They love their kids but find parenting challenging. And they care about kindness. They'll carpool to help time-poor school mums. They'll hold a stranger's baby to make it easier for them to wrangle a screaming toddler back into a pram. And they will never have the best handmade costume at Book Week, although they're happy for those who do. Half-arsed parents choose kinship and kindness over hashtags and humblebrags any day.

Chapter 17

THE SECRET OF HALF-ARSED PARENTING

This is a bloody hard time to be a parent. These days, a play date for a three-year-old involves 15 texts, three phone calls, an insurance policy check, a first-aid kit, a stop at the supermarket for allergy-appropriate snacks and two rides in the car. Over-parenting starts in infancy, when mums and dads carry baby monitors everywhere. These devices are meant to make parents more relaxed but actually make them more anxious because they can hear every sigh, squeak, fart and squeal. Phone apps allow parents to monitor their kids in childcare, keeping track of every piece of fruit consumed, drawing done and bowel moved. By school, kids are enrolled in every possible activity but given little time to get bored or make up games.

By high school, playgrounds are filled with kids sitting on mobile phones, Snapchatting the school's 'top ten fat girl list', playing 'Hot or Not' and logging onto RateMyTeacher.com. No one plays with yoyos, elastics or knuckles. When I was a kid, our butcher's son had real knuckles with little bits of flesh on them. You don't see that now. My generation was conceived in muscle cars and panel vans but hasn't lived up to the 70s' and 80s' sense of freedom and optimism.

Half-arsed parents need to tune out the bullshit and concentrate on the things that count. 'What's that?' I bet you're wondering. The short answer is: not as much as you'd think. British researchers surveyed 70,000 kids over a 70-year timeframe as part of the British Birth Cohorts study. In her brilliant book *The Life Project*, Helen Pearson pulled together findings from more than 6000 academic papers written from this data. She found that although class and money make a difference, parents and their kids can triumph despite a lack of funds and status. (Yay!) She found it is more important for parents to talk and listen to their kids and have ambitions for them than spend lots of money on them. It's also vital that parents are emotionally warm, teach their kids the alphabet and times tables, take them places, read to them, encourage them to read for pleasure and have regular bedtimes. Note there's no mention of the things modern parents are judged by, like the content of their kids' lunchboxes, their appearance at the school gate or how fancy their child's birthday party is.

These findings are reflected in an Australian survey of 10,000 primary school-aged kids. Associate Professor Rasheda Khanam from the University of Southern Queensland found richer kids do better at school, but they're not happier or better behaved than those from less privileged families. More important than money is a kid's home environment and the way their parents treat them and talk to them.

Khanam's study found cognitive development is affected by other things we can't control, like the child's birth weight, but also by things we *can* influence, like the number of books at home and engaging the child in cognitively stimulating activities. She found parental stress plays a key role: more stress has a negative effect on kids' behaviour and outlook. 'This is a positive finding for parents who don't have lots of money,' Khanam says. It's also a positive finding for half-arsed parents who are determined to stress less and enjoy parenting more.

There's reason to feel optimistic about the future. While Gen Zs and Gen Alpha may seem like self-centred prima donnas, there is every reason to believe their contribution to the world will extend beyond Justin Bieber and naked party aeroplane selfies. And despite all the terrible, awful, horrible no-good parenting out there, our kids love us. One study of more than 5000 Aussie kids aged eight to 14 found most children are close to their parents, relatives and friends. Yes, they're anxious, annoying and entitled, but we are the ones they turn to in a crisis. They love us and we love them.

Half-arsed parents aren't trying to be perfect, and that's why we accept our kids for the terrible and terrific people they are. They don't always make it easy on us. For instance, I am yet to convince my children to have showers because they need them, not just because they are told to have them. And the other day, I was having a fight with my daughter over how short her skirt was.

She wasn't about to take clothing advice from me. 'Mum, what would you know about fashion? Sometimes you don't even wear a bra around the house.' Hmmm, fair point.

For me, being a half-arsed parent is all about my 11-year-old son telling me he loves me 20 times a day. He's the one wondering whether dogs go through puberty and asking what happened to Pluto the planet. His latest creation is a cartoon featuring an intergalactic supercarrot who kills former US President Donald Trump. He's very smart. But the other day he changed my work email ID photo to a spirit wolf and no one knows how to turn it back. He's also the master of the 'fun fact' and asks endless questions like, 'Would you like to be queen of three nations or a God of two religions? Would you prefer to die by being eaten slowly by a million ants or fast by a lion?' (Not dying isn't usually an option.)

Half-arsed parenting for me is also about my 15-year-old daughter, who loves trying on all my clothes, plays me her favourite songs in the car and tells me all the goss, such as who got the dud bus buddy for the school excursion to Canberra. She's feisty, bold and brave. Even when she was only eight, she loved singing inappropriate teenage songs about drinking and getting laid in 7-Eleven parking lots. She looks better in my clothes than I do, is taller than me and says 'It's not like I am actually going to process that' when I ask why she's watching Netflix instead of doing her maths homework. When I ask her if she's done her teeth, she gives me a withering look, 'Obviously'. She and I spent isolation in our backyard laughing our heads off while doing exercise videos featuring women who appeared to get their work-out moves from third-rate strippers.

And it's about my 17-year-old son, who's taller than me but is still not too old for a hug – as long as none of his friends are around. He recently asked me if he could use my car to recreate a murder crime scene for his homework. (No.) The other day he said, 'Hey Mum, can you make my sandwich? It's a way for us to stay connected.' I think he was joking. For his sake, I hope he was joking. A few years ago, I took him on a fancy, expensive holiday. When we got home and he looked me in the eye – very heartfelt – and said, 'Thank you, Mum', I nearly choked up . . . then he finished. 'Thank you, Mum, for bringing me home to unlimited wi-fi.' He's driving now and has a job and I am proud of the strong, principled, kind young man he's become.

Half-arsed parenting tips

Half-arsed parents free their minds of stuff that doesn't matter. This means turning off the ticker-tape that's running inside their heads.

What will the other mums think if I don't volunteer for the school fete? (Who cares? If they judge you, they're not worth caring about.)

Will my son hate me if I buy the el cheapo mouthguard from the chemist instead of the $190 one in team colours? (Probably, but he did lose the last three you bought him.)

Am I a bad father because I've never once given my kids brown rice and kimchi for dinner? (No. Just because it looks good on someone's Insta feed, doesn't mean it's a good feed.)

Half-arsed parents have stopped looking for affirmation from others that's not going to come. They know there's no cheer squad waiting to applaud them for cooking yet another family dinner or working extra shifts to pay the bills. As Ashworth and Nobile write in *I Was a Really Good Mom Before I Had Kids*, 'When you are a mother, nobody's saying, "You're doing a great job, you're so great; what intuition, mopping up that vomit!"' Same goes for fathers, who rarely get thanked for battling peak hour traffic so they can spend ten hours a day at work. Where's their participation medal for that?

Half-arsed parents know it's important to feel joy and satisfaction in everyday life, and not just for the one week a year they spend drinking at a pool bar in Bali. They love their kids and want to enjoy raising them rather than feeling pressured and guilty all the time. This means they tune out the absurdity and hypocrisy of parenting experts who excuse bad behaviour from kids but demonise parents who wrap sandwiches in cling wrap or make phone calls while cooking dinner.

It's not for me to tell you what's going to make you feel good, but here are some of my favourite half-arsed strategies to get you started.

Listen to your children. My kids talk a lot, offering me loads of unsolicited advice. Don't sing, that dress makes your legs look weird, and why does your picture in the newspaper look nothing like you in real life? My daughter rarely holds back.

Me to her at 10.30 pm one school night: Why aren't
  you asleep?
Her: Why aren't YOU asleep?
Me: You are 14. That's why you should be asleep.
Her: *looks at me sadly, taking in my wrinkled face*
  You are 50. That's why YOU should be asleep.
(For the record, I am not 50 – yet.)

My younger son's not that much better.
Him: That's dope.
Me: Yeah, that's dope.
Him: *pauses and looks me up and down*
  It doesn't work if you're old.

But sometimes what my kids have to say is quite useful, such as pointing out that the person beeping me at the traffic lights for being too slow to take off (because I'd been texting) is a traffic cop.

Look after yourself. It's said that people without cancer want many things: more money in the bank, better behaved children and a guilt-free way to eat chocolate. People with cancer want one thing: to be cancer-free. Only those who have been truly unwell understand the value of health. The rest of us obsess about silly things such as forgetting to bring recyclable bags to the supermarket and spending $45 on runny French cheese. Recently spending five days sweating over the results of a breast scan reminded me to value my healthy body, which still has all its original moving parts.

Throw a party. When was the last time you threw a really great party – not for the kids, for you? It doesn't matter what the event is. Celebrate one year on from divorce with a mock hen's night with penis-shaped pasta and sex-toy table decorations. Celebrate losing ten kilos with a clothes-swap party with friends. Celebrate summer by putting blow-up pools on the back lawn and inviting everyone over. When friends say they don't want any fuss made of their milestone birthdays, find a way to make it special anyway.

Music is your friend. If the last time you bought an album was on a cassette, CD or LP, then it's time to blow out the musical cobwebs. A few years ago, I found myself in a very quiet house after the children spent their first weekend with their dad at his house. So, I invited a whole lot of musical friends called Adele, Justin, Katy and Taylor over. I pumped up the volume and sang as loud as I wanted. Half-arsed parents dance like no one is watching, even though the kids are secretly filming us in the hope they'll have a viral hit on their hands.

Wear the bathing suit. I've got one friend who spent years sitting on the beach watching her husband and kids swim because she didn't like the look of her body in bathers. Then one day she wore the suit and guess what happened? Nothing. No one put up 'beached whale' signs, no one stared, no one even cared.

Half-arsed parents don't worry about what others think of the size of their arse or gut, and concentrate on something they can control, like finding a decent swimsuit they feel good in.

Wear the pasta necklace. On birthdays, Mother's Day and Father's Day, parents should expect to be seen in public wearing the most ridiculous accessories made by their children. These may include pasta necklaces, hats made out of ice-cream containers and finger-knitted scarves. Half-arsed parents proudly wear them all (but don't feel guilty taking them off as soon as the kids are out of sight). Remember finger knitting? That is what passed as fun before the internet was invented.

Let the kids wear what they want. Half-arsed parents allow their kids to make their own fashion and decorating mistakes. Offering advice like, 'You may regret painting your walls black' or 'Have you looked in a full-length mirror?' is bound to backfire. You may need to be patient with your female teen. A decision involving which of five identical pairs of white jeans she's going to wear to a party involves no less than 15 texts, two phone calls, 67 DMs and a class-wide Snapchat discussion.

Things do get easier. Half-arsed parents know they will one day celebrate their kids being old enough to sit through an entire meal without playing noughts and crosses on the table-cloth, going on endless trips to the toilet or taking 458 snaps of their knee with an iPhone. There is a turning point when parents stop trying to make their kids be quiet and instead try and make them talk.

In the blink of an eye they go from, 'Muuum, Muuum, Muuum, I'm thirsty, Muuum, Muuum, Muuum, I'm hungry,' to, 'Muuum, Muuum, Muuum, can I have $50?'.

Mistakes don't matter. Half-arsed parents like me know this all too well. I took my three kids to the dentist on Tuesday at 8.30 am on a school day. We walked in a bit early after being in a mad rush to be there on time. The receptionist said: 'What are you doing here?' We were three minutes and seven days early for the appointment. We celebrated with hot chocolate and jam croissants.

Have a date night. Go out with your partner, parent or great friend regularly and don't talk about interest rates or car insurance, but fun topics like how crazy the kids would be if you cancelled Netflix. I love my partner and our crazy, fun family life filled with my kids, his kids, his mum, my mum, his friends, my friends, our friends, our siblings, their kids and everyone else. But I also love time spent just with him.

Perfection is impossible. I scribbled notes at the back of *I Was a Really Good Mom Before I Had Kids* about a bad dinner I prepared many years ago. It was a recipe from *Deceptively Delicious* by Jessica Seinfeld – probably macaroni and cheese with pureed butternut squash or some other secret healthy ingredient. It sounded simple but took ages to cook. My kids hated it and wouldn't eat it.

I cracked it because I'd put so much effort into it. The meal wasn't for them; it was for me. I was showing I could be the perfect mother. The night ended with me in tears and my daughter tired, hungry and disoriented. I remember singing her to sleep. My son was hungry too and kept asking me, 'Are you happy with me?'. I felt like a failure because I tried to be something I wasn't. We would all have been better off with a tin of baked beans with grated cheese on it.

Wine is an answer, but not a solution. Half-arsed parents love receiving cards that say, 'Your children should always be your inspiration, even if it is just to drink more' or 'May your to-do list be empty and your wine glass stay full'. But most of us are trying to drink less than we once did.

Keep the best of your isolation life going. When Covid hit, the world slowly shut down. No more cars on the streets. No more kids at school. No more people at work. No more toilet paper on the shelves. We retreated to the safety (and insanity) of our homes to lick cake mix directly from the beaters and write SAVE ME FROM MY KIDS on chalk on the pavement. Yes, it was hard having everyone under one roof and co-ordinating home schooling and work. But it wasn't all bad. There were no early-morning netball games, no endless drop-offs, no boring commutes, no traffic jams. In our neighbourhood there were rainbows on the footpaths, teddy bears in the windows and families playing together in parks. When kids were forced to unplug from their digital devices, you could see them out riding bikes with their friends, playing board games with their siblings and enjoying the freedom of nothing to do and lots of time to do it in. Half-arsed parents want to keep the best of isolation going – the family togetherness and games – while blocking out any memory of the night they had to use newspaper in the dunny.

It's time to be half-arsed

For a long time, we've needed a new model of raising kids that takes the stress off kids and parents and lets us all enjoy life again. This is it. It's time to free yourself as a parent. Let go of hyper-parenting, helicopter parenting, cottonwool parenting and hands-on parenting, and embrace half-arsed parenting. Half-arsed parents are happy to be good enough. They tune out the crazies, trust their instincts and channel 70s dads who pick their kids up from parties late at night wearing terry towelling bathrobes.

Half-arsed parents cut down their time on social media if looking at the amazing lives others lead – or pretend to – makes them feel like crap. I will never be a picture-perfect social media mum. The idea of showcasing my fabulous life to others doesn't appeal to half-arsed parents like me. I make this promise to you all. I will not share photos of me doing burpees while holding one or more children on my lap. I might do burps, but not burpees. I will not put hashtags before any of these words: pure, strong, young, blessed or inspiration. And I will not post endless photos of my perfectly dressed children and immaculate house with beds decorated with multiple colour-coded pillows and hand-knitted designer throws. The only throw on my bed is likely to be throw-up.

Half-arsed parents are determined to return to the time when kids playing alone in the park was normal, not worthy of a human services check. When children were naughty and punished, rather than their parents. When you could share food at school when someone forgot their lunch. When you could have parties without asking the whole class in case someone got left out. When parents went to the hospital emergency department because someone had a piece of Lego up their nose, not because they hurt their hand playing soccer. When kids learnt to drive in shopping centre car parks on Sundays. And when weekends were about parents, not getting kids to sporting events and play dates.

Half-arsed parents want to raise their kids in a world without Nude Food Days and kids' lunchboxes with fiddly little built-in freezer bricks. They unwrap their kids from cottonwool, de-plug them and let them be free. They take their kids to the park and leave them there. They let them hang out, go exploring, have adventures and have fun without being watched over by an adult. When the kids have had enough (or you've had enough of them moaning about what they're missing online), they hand them screens so everyone can have a break.

Half-arsed parenting is a clarion call against the assumption that our children need protection, not freedom. Half-arsed parents aren't taking things so seriously that they forget to have a life filled with kindness, dancing, fun and happiness. We are fighting back against those who want to ban or modify anything that could cause harm or challenge our kids. And we sure as hell can cope with book characters called Dick and Fanny.

Letting go allows half-arsed parents to concentrate on the big parenting issues, like whether their child is having mental health problems, taking drugs, falling behind at school or joining the Young Liberals. But it also gives them a chance to nail some important, radical, life-changing things, like being happy, being kind and taking care of all the people in their lives that matter – like parents and friends – and not just the kids.

For half-arsed parents, this may mean giving kids canteen money rather than making one more bloody school lunch. Or paying people to do jobs they hate like washing the inside of the car, ironing and watching the Logies. For me, it's refusing to holiday at a campsite with communal showers, buying my own birthday presents so I get exactly what I want and saying no more often to my kids. Oh, and making sure my car never becomes a fake murder crime scene.

Half-arsed parents don't have the time, energy or money to worry about how important it is to 'be vulnerable' in the hope that 'beautiful things will happen' like some celebrities. Winning $50 on a scratchie, finding out the mole on their arm isn't cancerous and getting a new baby to sleep for more than 15 minutes at a time is about as beautiful as it gets in half-arsed households.

Half-arsed parents don't have a fitness routine. They're happy enough to duck around the block with the dog after dinner three nights a week. They don't have a fashion philosophy. They buy the clothes they can afford. And they don't have a home decoration plan. They have a house with some furniture in it and knick-knacks they were given for wedding presents and haven't sold on eBay yet. Half-arsed parents don't have a lifestyle – they have a life, and a damned good one at that.

Half-arsed parents don't need celebrities, bloggers or Insta influencers advising them. They trust their gut because they know most of the answers anyway. They free themselves from the guilt, expectation and pressure from others and accept that good enough is more than enough. In fact, it's great. Half-arsed parents don't have to be perfect. The key is to set low standards that are met most of the time. And if they aren't, it won't matter. No one will notice and no one will care. The kids will be happier because their parents are happier.

Remember: have a laugh, keep it real and don't judge others too harshly. They're probably like you and doing their best. Live the life you want and assess your success by your happiness, not your kid's achievements. Make everyone twice as satisfied by doing half as much. Half-arsed parents know there's no need to be unhappy about the way their children are being brought up because they're the ones raising them. They know they have the power to change things.

In my household, it's a work in progress – there are still too many sporting matches, too much Netflix and too much attitude from the little buggers, but we're getting there. Indeed, it's fair to say my half-arsed parenting is, well, half-arsed. I'm only halfway there, and that's okay.

Good luck with your half-arsed parenting adventures. As I said in the beginning, drop your standards, ditch the guilt and relax. This book is your participation medal – for achievement, not effort. You may not have an Insta-worthy lifestyle, but at least you can have a life filled with love, laughter and Vegemite pasta whenever you damn well please. It all comes down to tuning out the bullshit and focusing on what really matters – staying sane and raising happy kids who aren't dickheads.

Half-arsed golden rules

1. Doing half as much is more than enough.

2. Adopt a 'she'll be right' attitude because mostly it is.

3. Pick your battles – give in occasionally but don't give up.

4. Keep the kids safe and alive long enough to fund your old age.

5. Ignore bad advice. You know when it's bad, so go with your gut.

6. You don't need to be a tech-free, hands-free parent. You're doing just fine with your hands full.

7. Don't believe everyone who says they feel #blessed on social media. They're probably #fullofshit.

8. Cut corners, diminish expectations and underwhelm your loved ones at every opportunity.

9. Drop your standards, ditch the guilt and relax.

10. Give yourself a participation medal – for achievement rather than effort.

And remember:

>Just because it's on, you don't have to go.

>Just because it exists, you don't need to have it.

>Just because the kids want it, you don't have to buy it.

>Just because they ask you, you don't have to say yes.

>Take care of yourself the way you take care of everyone else.

Feel better? Good.

SELECTED READING

Here is a selection of the resources I have used in my research. A full list of endnotes is available online at murdochbooks.com.au; just search for *The Secret of Half-arsed Parenting*.

Books

Ainsworth, T. & Noble, A., *I Was a Really Good Mom Before I Had Kids: Reinventing Modern Motherhood*, Chronicle Books, New York, 2010.

The Australian Women's Weekly, *Children's Birthday Cake Book: Vintage edition*, Bauer Media, 2011.

Benedictus, L., McUtchen, A. & Macvean, J., *The Father Hood*, Murdoch Books, Sydney, 2019.

Berry, K., *Family, Food and Feelings*, Pan Macmillan, Sydney, 2019.

Bort, J., Pflock, A., Renner, D., *Mommy Guilt: Learn to worry less, focus on what matters and raise happy kids*, Amacom, USA, 2005.

Carr-Gregg, M. & Robinson, E., *The Princess Bitchface Syndrome 2.0*, Penguin, Sydney, 2017.

Carr-Gregg, M. & Robinson, E., *The Prince Boofhead Syndrome*, Penguin, Sydney, 2017.

Coulson, J., *Miss-connection: Why Your Teenage Daughter 'Hates' You, Expects the World and Needs to Talk*, ABC Books, Sydney, 2020.

Crabb, A., *The Wife Drought*, Penguin, Sydney, 2015.

DeBenedet, A.T., & Cohen, L.J., *The Art of Roughhousing: Good Old-Fashioned Horseplay and Why Every Kid Needs It*, Quirk Books, Philadelphia, 2011.

Deedley, S., *Positive Parenting: Parenthood: Become the Parents that Children Love to Spend Time With*, independently published, 2017.

Douglas, S. J. & Michaels, M. W., *The Mommy Myth: The Idealization of Motherhood and How It Has Undermined All Women*, Free Press, New York, 2004.

Dubois, L., *You Will (Probably) Survive: And Other Things They Don't Tell You About Motherhood*, Allen & Unwin, Sydney, 2019.

Ford, G., *The Contented Mother's Guide*, Random House, London, 2012.

Freedman, M., *Work Strife Balance*, Macmillan Australia, Sydney, 2017.

Freedman, M., *Mama Mia: A Memoir of Mistakes, Magazines and Motherhood*, Harper Collins, Sydney, 2009.

Fuller, A., *Tricky Teens: How to Create a Great Relationship with Your Teen... Without Going Crazy!* Finch Publishing, Sydney, 2014.

Goodwin, Kristy, *Raising Your Child in a Digital World: What you Really Need to Know!* Finch Publishing, Sydney, 2016.

Gorr, L., *The A-Z of Mummy Manners: An Etiquette Guide for Managing Other Children's Mothers and Assorted Mummy Dilemmas*, Harper Collins, Sydney, 2011.

Greagen, C. *Reservoir Dad: He's got it covered*, Random House Australia, Sydney, 2014.

Judd, Rebecca, *The Baby Bible: Taking Care of Your Bump, Your Baby and Yourself*, Allen and Unwin, Sydney, *2018.*

Kilmartin, L., Moline, K., Ybarbo, A., & Zoellner, M., *Sh*tty Mum: The Guide for Good Enough Mums,* Hodder, London, 2012.

King, M., *Being 14: Helping fierce teens become awesome women*, Hachette Australia, Sydney, 2017.

Laditan, B., *The Honest Toddler: A Child's Guide to Parenting*, Orion Books, London, 2013.

Laditan, B., *Toddlers are A**holes: It's Not your Fault*, Workman Publishing, New York, 2015.

Locke, J. Y., *The Bonsai Child: Why modern parenting limits children's potential and practical strategies to turn it around*, Judith Locke, Kelvin Grove, 2015.

Marsden, J., *The Art of Growing Up*, Macmillan Australia, Sydney, 2019.

Marshall, B., *The Tech Diet for Your Child & Teen: 7-step Plan to Reclaim Your Kid's Childhood (and Your Family's Sanity)*, Harper Collins, Sydney, 2019.

McCready, A., *The Me, Me, Me Epidemic: A Step-by-Step Guide to Raising Capable, Grateful Kids in an Over-Entitled World*, Penguin, New York, 2016.

Passmore, S., *Parenting for a Happier Home*, Exile Publishing, Sydney, 2016.

Pearson, H., *The Life Project: The Story of 70,000 Ordinary Lives*, Soft Skull Press, London, 2016.

Robertson, B., *Hear Me Roar: The Story of a Stay-at-Home Dad*, University of Queensland Press, Brisbane, 2012.

Rosenfeld, A., *The Over-Scheduled Child: Avoiding the Hyper-Parenting Trap*, St Martin's Press, New York, 2001.

Rowe, J., *Diary of a Crap Housewife: It's Time to Embrace Your Perfectly Imperfect Life*, Allen and Unwin, Sydney, 2019.

Silverstone, A., *The Kind Mama: A Simple Guide to Supercharged Fertility, a Radiant Pregnancy, a Sweeter Birth, and a Healthier, More Beautiful Beginning*, Rodale Press, USA, 2013.

Stafford, R. M., *Hands Free Mama: A Guide to Putting Down the Phone, Burning the To-Do List, and Letting Go of Perfection to Grasp What Really Matters!*, Zondervan, Michigan, USA, 2014.

Walker, K., *Future-Proofing your Child: Help your children grow into sensible, safe, happy, resilient, self-motivated teens and beyond*, Penguin, Sydney, 2015.

Waters, Lea, *The Strength Switch*, Random House, Sydney, 2017.

West, Madeleine, *Six Under Eight: When Parenting Becomes an Extreme Sport*, Penguin, Sydney, 2016.

White, Shannon Kelly, *Parenting for Legends*, Bad Girls Media, Melbourne, 2018.

Winnicott, Donald, *Playing and Reality*, Tavistock Publications, London, 1971.

Research reports

Australian Bureau of Statistics, *Gender Indicators*, September 2017.

Australian Child Wellbeing Project, *Are the kids alright? Young Australians in Their Middle Years: Final Report*, 2016.

Australian Centre on Quality of Life, *Australian Unity Wellbeing Index: Middle-Aged Australians in a Wellbeing Funk*, 2018.

Australian Institute of Family Studies (AIFS), *The Modern Australian Family*, 2019.

AIFS, *Young people living with their parents*, 2019.

AIFS, *Stay-at-home dads: Families Week Fact Sheet*, 2017.

AIFS, *Growing Up in Australia Longitudinal Study of Australian Children Annual Statistical Report*, 2017.

AIFS, *Longitudinal Study of Australian Children Annual Statistical Report*, 2016.

AIFS, *Life Satisfaction across Life Course Transitions: Australian Family Trends,* 2015.

AIFS, *Mother's Day Fact Sheet,* 2016.

Australian Institute of Health and Welfare, *Overweight and Obesity,* 2019.

Commonwealth of Australia, *The Mental Health of Children and Adolescents: Report on the second Australian Child and Adolescent Survey of Mental Health and Wellbeing, 2015.*

Jean Hailes for Women's Health, *Women's Health Survey,* 2018.

The Lego Foundation, *Play Well Report,* Denmark, 2018.

National Centre for Social and Economic Modelling, *Race Against Time: How Australians Spend their Time,* 2011.

Parenting Research Centre (PRC), *Focus on Fathers,* 2018.

PRC, *Parenting Today in Victoria: Technical Report,* 2017.

Real Insurance, *Family Values* report, 2019.

Journals

Academic Pediatrics

Australian and New Zealand Journal of Psychiatry

Australian Journal of Guidance and Counselling

Australian Journal of Psychologists and Counsellors in Schools

BMC Public Health

Body Image

Child Abuse and Neglect

Children and Youth Services Review

Current Opinion in Psychology

Demography

Developmental Psychology

Discourse, Context & Media

Drug and Alcohol Dependence

Emotion, Space and Society

Family Matters

Health and Place

Infant Behaviour and Development

International Journal of Behavioural Nutrition and Physical Activity

Journal of Medical Internet Research

Journal of Nutrition, Education and Behaviour

Journal of Paediatrics and Child Health
Journal of Transport Geography
Leisure Sciences
Medical Journal of Australia
Pediatrics
Personality and Adjustment
Social Media + Society
Social Science and Medicine
Women and Birth

ACKNOWLEDGEMENTS

I would like to thank Edwina Jamieson for suggesting I write a book like this many years ago. (Sorry it took me three kids and 12 years to get around to it.)

Thank you to my agent Bernadette Foley who made it all happen. Thank you also to my Murdoch Books team of Lou Johnson, Jane Morrow, Virginia Birch and Libby Turner. Nice work, ladies! It's been fun!

Thanks to my school-mum buddies, work buddies and family members for keeping me sane. Thanks to Claire, Rebecca and Janey for the Friday sessions and walks during lockdown. Love you, girls.

And thank you to Elissa Hunt, the former *Herald Sun* digital editor, whose talk of a 'half-arsed Christmas' sparked the idea for the column that led to this book.

Susie O'Brien is a journalist and columnist with a PhD in Education. For the last 19 years she has written about parenting and social issues for the *Adelaide Advertiser* and *Herald Sun* newspapers, and she appears weekly on Channel Seven's *Sunrise*. She and her partner together have five kids – they're the Brady Bunch, without Alice to help hold it all together.